Biblical Preaching
for Contemporary Man

Biblical Preaching
for
Contemporary Man

Compiled by
Neil B. Wiseman

BAKER BOOK HOUSE
Grand Rapids, Michigan

PHOTOLITHOPRINTED BY CUSHING - MALLOY, INC.
ANN ARBOR, MICHIGAN, UNITED STATES OF AMERICA
1977

Contents

Preface

"He hasn't said anything yet." Those were the words of the missionary translator to his people during the opening of the visiting preacher's sermon. Those words could very well be from the people who listen in some places to present-day preaching. But such a remark is never accurate when the preacher is a true biblical preacher. That is what this book is all about.

The church in the late seventies is alive with talk about preaching. Joking, criticism, and in some places gladness is being expressed about preaching. So there is hope, because those who judge or joke have some small vision of what preaching ought to be, and those who rejoice are being challenged afresh by the Bible through their preacher. That is what this book is all about.

Biblical Preaching for Contemporary Man is written by nine practicing preachers—six of them pastors. When they were asked to contribute to this symposium on preaching, their immediate reply was "Yes—happy to!" Such a wholehearted response is a good sign for preaching's future. These writers believe sound biblical preaching is here to stay because contemporary man wants to hear a fresh word from God creatively applied to his life. That is what this book is all about.

This book has been produced basically for the Pastors Leadership Conferences (PALCON) which are sponsored by the Board of General Superintendents of the Church of the Nazarene. To all who read, let the challenge go forth again, "Preach the Word!" And do so with the firm assurance that such preaching will produce new converts, strong Christians, and noble churches.

— NEIL B. WISEMAN
PALCON, 1976

● **W. T. Purkiser**

1

What Is Biblical Preaching?

With all the changes time has brought to the work of the ministry, preaching is still its major function. Today's pastor may be a counsellor, an educator, an administrator, and a promoter. But if he is to fulfill his God-called purpose, he is first of all a preacher. Preaching is not the pastor's only work, but it is his most important work.

Many reasons may be given for the importance of preaching. Not the least is the one stated by the Apostle Paul: "It pleased God by the foolishness of preaching to save them that believe" (1 Cor. 1:21). True preaching is more than the recitation of truth. Preaching is the extension into our time of that saving and sanctifying work of Christ which is the essence of the gospel. When the Word is preached in faith, as Emil Brunner long since said, the most important happening on the face of the earth takes place.

To preach is more than to say words. Preaching is an

act of God through a human being in which the redemptive work of Christ becomes present reality. It is the faithful proclamation of the message of the Bible in such a way that ancient truth becomes modern trauma and triumph.

Preaching not only says something, it does something. To preach is to become part of the mission of Christ who came "to seek and to save that which was lost" (Luke 19:10). It is to bring the Cross and the Resurrection out of the past into the present moment of decision.

True preaching brings the historic Incarnation into the modern occasion. In effect, it reenacts the redemptive event it describes. The risen Redeemer becomes the contemporary Christ, the living Lord who confronts people today with His decisive call, "Follow me." Ancient fact becomes living reality in the Spirit-anointed preaching of the Word. Through preaching, Christ judges, saves, teaches, and directs us in this our day as surely as He judged, saved, taught, and directed those He met in Galilee and Judaea 1,900 years ago.

In true preaching, the words of a man become the Word of God. God speaks and acts directly in human life. J. B. Phillips translates 2 Cor. 5:20, "We are now Christ's ambassadors, as though God were appealing direct to you through us." What begins as an encounter person to person between the man in the pulpit and the people in the pew becomes an encounter Person to person in which the man in the pulpit drops out of sight and God through His Spirit individually addresses those who hear.

What then Rome claims for the Mass, Protestants possess in the "sacrament" of the Spirit-directed preaching—the reenactment of the redeeming sacrifice of Christ.

A student asked his homiletics professor, "Prof, will my sermon do?"

The real question is the response of the professor: "Do what?"

10

Whatever else this means—and what it means has been set forth in eloquent detail by Peter Forsyth, Herbert Farmer, James S. Stewart, Donald G. Miller, John Knox, and others[1]—it means that preaching is not what it ought to be unless it is in a real sense biblical preaching. *Gospel* is a word that means "God's spell"—literally, "God's story"—and God's story is told nowhere else with such strength and purity as in the Book His Spirit inspired.

What Biblical Preaching Is

Unfortunately, much modern preaching falls far short of what it should be. It is little more than religious editorializing on the life and thought of modern man. Such moralizing has brought preaching into the kind of disrepute suggested in the retort "Don't you preach at me. I've had enough of your preaching." Preaching is reduced to the level of scolding.

It takes little insight to see what has happened. Such preaching has lost its biblical rootage. God judges but He does not scold. Instead of "Thus saith the Lord," the theme of preaching of this sort is "Thus saith the latest book I've read," or worse, "Thus saith the latest notion I've had." Only a biblical vision of what preaching should be, and only preaching that is truly biblical, can win the hearing the Church must have if it is to survive and succeed in today's world.

Preaching may be biblical in two ways: when its content is biblical, when it proclaims what the Bible teaches; and when it is biblical in form, when it takes its direction from and expounds the thought of a biblical passage.

This means that not all biblical preaching is textual or expository. Indeed, some alleged textual and expository preaching is decidedly unbiblical. But all biblical preaching roots in the meaning and message of the Bible itself.

Topical preaching may be biblical—if the topic is explored in the light of the balanced teaching of the Scriptures. Topical preaching puts greater responsibility on the preacher to insure that its content and development is truly in harmony with the whole message of the Bible. Preaching is biblical when what is preached is what the Scriptures teach. Each point must be examined to be sure it expresses biblical truth, and each point should be supported by direct scriptural reference.

But biblical preaching takes on an added dimension of power and depth when even its form is shaped by the biblical passage explored. The Bible becomes not only a guide to *what* is preached but *how* it is preached. Here, textual and expository preaching takes advantage of the way the truth is presented in the Scriptures. Its biblical roots are both real and obvious.

With no circularity intended, the preaching described in the Bible is biblical preaching. The prophets of the Old Testament consistently prefaced their oracles with "Thus saith the Lord." The New Testament characteristically identifies preaching the gospel with "preaching the word." Jesus "preached the word unto them" (Mark 2:2). People never thought of Him as a priest but always as "one of the prophets" (Matt. 16:14), proclaiming the Word of God. Over and over throughout the Book of Acts, the work of the apostles is described as "preaching the word" (Acts 8:4, 25; 11:19; 13:4; 14:25; 15:35–36; 16:6; 17:13). Paul urges Timothy—and all who follow—to "preach the word; be instant in season and out of season; reprove, rebuke, exhort with all longsuffering and doctrine" (2 Tim. 4:2).

There is, to be sure, a wooden, mechanical, legalistic use of the Bible that is dutiful but not dynamic. But preaching that takes a biblical passage or theme, explores its implications, and applies its message, cannot fail to accomplish the purposes for which God sends forth His Word.

Biblical preaching may move in either of two directions. It may select and announce a specific passage and authentically apply its truth to the lives of the hearers. Or it may start with a recognized problem and turn to the Bible for its answer. Today's preaching, as Karl Barth once suggested, must look at life with the Bible in one hand and a newspaper in the other.

As there is a plan unfolding throughout the Bible, so biblical preaching ideally is planned preaching. The plans are as varied as the men who make them. The important thing is that there be a plan. Plans, of course, are subject to change by the Holy Spirit who (it is hoped) first suggested them. But the preacher who plans his pulpit work six months or a year ahead and who keeps that plan always in mind has half his preparation already done. Sermons planned in advance can grow, and to *grow* sermons is always better than building them.

Preaching plans may involve series—preaching through the Bible book by book, chapter by chapter, paragraph by paragraph, a series of great themes, passages, or personalities. They may involve "courses" of sermons—related to the preaching aims of the minister himself, although not announced as a series.

Part of planning for the future should be a review of the past. What subjects, what emphases, have been covered in the past year? If the hearers had only this one pulpit ministry from which to form their understanding of Christianity, what sort of faith would they have? What important Bible themes have been covered? More apropos, what important Bible themes have been passed over? But whatever the plan, and however it be formulated, what is important is that there be one.

The Advantages of Biblical Preaching

Much of the value of biblical preaching is implied in what has already been said. Its specific advantages may now at least briefly be listed. There are advantages for the listener. And there are advantages for the preacher.

1. *Biblical preaching assists in building an enduring and spiritually mature church.* Several studies of outstanding churches have been made in recent years. It is interesting to note the number of them in which the preaching is described in such statements as: "The preaching was a simple exposition of a biblical passage"; or "There was a good deal of scriptural reference in the sermon, and much direct application to the problems which beset the ordinary person."

Why should we think people prefer our speculations to the declaration of God's Word? Why should we think we can attract a hearing by substituting popularized psychology, philosophy, or politics for the Scriptures?

People come to church not to hear some novel idea, not to get more information about world events, not even to be informed about the achievements of their own particular religious group. They come to hear some sure word of God—something that will illumine life to its core, and send them out with lifted vision, broadened horizons, a more sure hope, and the purified determination to do the will of God as He makes it known to them. To give them anything other than such a word is to offer stones for bread or a serpent for fish.

Biblical preaching educates the congregation in the essentials of sound doctrine. For many moderns, the Bible is little more than "a housing project for bookworms." Rarely will the level of biblical knowledge in the pew surpass that in the pulpit. The spiritual illiteracy of the present day will be cured, if at all, by a thoroughly biblical pastoral ministry.

2. *Biblical preaching stimulates variety in the pastor's ministry.* Faithfully and systematically to preach the Bible is to find an infinite variety of themes and their development. It is impossible to become a faddist or ride a hobby when one conscientiously preaches the whole counsel of God.

Ended forever is the pastor's frantic search for sermon topics. Before him is a Source Book for preaching that is unlimited in its breadth and scope. His "seedbed" of texts and topics will be as prolific as nature's production of seeds—far beyond the minimum necessary to sustain the life of the species.

The faithful study and preaching of any portion of God's Word will yield a wide variety of basic themes and applications to every conceivable need of human life. Practical duties will be impressed on Christian hearers, not because they are selected at the whim of the preacher, but because they emerge in his faithful exposition of the Scriptures. The warnings as well as the promises of the Bible will be expounded, not dragged in by the heels, so to speak, but as they are encountered in the Word itself.

3. *Biblical preaching keeps the pulpit down to earth and practical.* There is no ivory tower in the Scriptures. The purpose of the Bible is "doctrine, . . . reproof, . . . correction, . . . [and] instruction in righteousness: that the man of God may be perfect, throughly furnished unto all good works" (2 Tim. 3:16–17).

Sometimes preaching *about* the Bible is confused with biblical preaching. Preaching about the Bible may indeed be abstract, technical, and without much spiritual value. But, as John Knox insists, when preaching is authentic, it is relevant. If it lacks relevance, it is not truly

15

biblical. We do not, as some have said, "Make the Bible live." What we do is make its life apparent—turn it loose in the world to do the work of God.

4. *Biblical preaching encourages the minister's unceasing personal study of the Bible.* He must become, in John Wesley's phrase, "a man of one Book." This will not mean for him—any more than it meant for Wesley—that he reads nothing but the Bible. It will mean that everything he reads, and the vital focus of his interest, will always be brought to the measuring rod of the Scriptures.

Preaching can be biblical only to the degree that the preacher himself first wrestles with the passage he preaches. In its meticulous study he finds not only food for his people but the enrichment of his own understanding of the Word.

Along with careful and intensive study of parts of the Bible, the preacher must combine a consistent program for the study of the whole—the sweeping, overall grasp of biblical theology that saves one from a limited and parochial view. Neglect of Bible study inevitably dries up the springs of inspiration and power. "Lifelong learning" must be the slogan in the preacher's personal Bible study.

5. *Biblical preaching imparts authority to the pulpit.* It restores the prophetic note to preaching. The ultimate authority of the preacher is not his education, his scholarship, his experience, his natural wisdom; it is "Thus saith the Lord." The amazement of the people who listened to the Sermon on the Mount was not at the novelty of Christ's teachings. It was that "he taught them as one having authority, and not as the scribes" (Matt. 7:29). This authority our Lord shares with those who preach His Word.

True, the preacher must not confuse his private interpretations of the Word with the authority of God.

"Pulpit infallibility" is no more a reality than "papal infallibility." The preacher must never let the fact that he stands "three feet above contradiction" invest him with a dogmatic and unbending mentality. The authority of the Word is not that of individual or sectarian interpretation; it is the authority of Christ shining through the truth however imperfectly presented.

The Preparation for Biblical Preaching

It is possible to give lip service to biblical preaching without ever getting down to the hard labor involved. A biblical preacher needs tools, just as a carpenter needs tools; but having the tools makes a man neither a preacher nor a carpenter unless he learns to use them.

Whatever the exceptions, biblical preaching starts from a passage of scripture—a verse or, better, a paragraph. In any case, the scripture selected should include enough of the context to give all the facets of the thought. The selected passage will have a meaning almost immediately apparent, but it must still be thoroughly studied. The hidden treasure of its deepest truth will be yielded up only as the preacher lives with it, wrestles with its words and phrases, reads it through again and again, and studies it carefully.

Access to the original Hebrew and Greek texts is valuable but not necessary. A preacher with little or no knowledge of either biblical language can learn to use interlinear translations as by Marshall; analytical concordances by Young and Strong; word studies by Barclay, Richardson, Robertson and, more recently, Earle; Vine's *Expository Dictionary of New Testament Words*; as well as a wealth of contemporary translations.

Only after he has made a firsthand study of the passage should the preacher turn to the commentaries: the

Beacon Bible Commentary; *Beacon Bible Expositions*; Barclay's *Daily Bible Study*; *The New Bible Commentary*; Adam Clarke and Matthew Henry; *The Interpreter's Bible*; and the large number of commentaries on individual books—the *International Critical Commentaries*; *The New International Commentary*; Moffatt's, Epworth, Tyndale, Torch, and Harper's, to name some of the leaders.

Basic to biblical preaching is what is technically called exegesis, or more broadly, hermeneutics—the art of discovering and defining the meaning of the biblical text. The biblical preacher must know and apply the basic principles of interpretation.

Interpretation deals with the meanings of sentences. One writer has given as the golden rule of biblical preaching:

> *Make some scripture statement the basis of your*
> *   message:*
> *Know what it means:*
> *Preach what it says:...*
> *The meaning of a passage is never ours to decide,*
> *   but only ours to discover.*[2]

Some principles may be suggested for the discovery of meanings.

1. *Start with the assumption that the Bible is God's Word, and that it speaks to the human predicament today.* It is not one book among others; it is *the* Book.

This means that considerations of a critical nature, valid as they may be, belong to the study and not the pulpit. The preacher may wrestle with questions; he must preach answers. This gives point to W. R. Maltby's comment that although the well is deep and the preacher

18

needs a long rope to draw the water, he should not make the people "chew on the rope."

For all its humanness, the Bible is divine. It "inerrantly [reveals] the will of God concerning us in all things necessary to our salvation." We do not judge it; it judges us. It is not that we "go through the Bible"; the Bible must go through us. It is the "given" with which we start. We are not called to change it or even to defend it but to proclaim it.

This means appreciation for the spiritual factor in Bible study. The Word is spiritually discerned. The Holy Spirit as Teacher is the prime essential. The preacher enters his study with Clara Scott's prayer:

> *Open my eyes, that I may see*
> *Glimpses of truth Thou hast for me;*
> *Place in my hands the wonderful key*
> *That shall unclasp, and set me free.*
> *Silently now I wait for Thee,*
> *Ready, my God, Thy will to see.*
> *Open my eyes, illumine me,*
> *Spirit divine.*

2. *Give specific attention to the literary form.* This is a frame of reference logically prior to the words themselves. The Bible embraces many literary forms: poetry, proverbial wisdom, history, chronicle, sermon, oracle, parable, allegory, and epistle.

Each literary form obviously involves principles of interpretation proper to itself. "The Lord is my rock" does not mean that God is granite or limestone. "He shall cover thee with his feathers, and under his wings shalt thou trust" is not evidence that God is a Being with wings and feathers.

Less obvious are expressions sometimes known as Hebraisms. An example would be comparisons stated in

19

absolute terms. "Hate" may mean a lesser degree of love, as when Jesus said, "If any man come to me, and hate not his father, and mother, and wife, and children, and brethren, and sisters, yea, and his own life also, he cannot be my disciple" (Luke 14:26). "Labour not for the meat which perisheth, but for that meat which endureth unto everlasting life" (John 6:27) does not forbid earning one's daily bread but stresses the greater value of spiritual food.

Other examples would include the "prophetic present" in which Isaiah 9:6 says, "Unto us a child is born, unto us a son is given," when the event itself was 700 years in the future; and Paul says, "Whom he did predestinate, them he also called: and whom he called, them he also justified: and whom he justified, them he also glorified" (Rom. 8:30), when the glorification is yet to come. In a similar way, biblical writers often speak of what is certain as if it were close at hand although it may be yet distant in point of time.

One marvels at the confusion caused by the typical Hebraic expression for a short time, "three days and three nights." This is used once for Christ's stay in the tomb, and there are those who declare that it must mean a literal 72 hours—although all four Gospels declare the Crucifixion to have been on "the preparation," the regular Greek term for Friday; and the New Testament says 16 times that Christ was raised from the dead "the third day."

3. *Study the key words of the passage under consideration.* Don't be too sure you know what they mean. Individual words are the ultimate units of meaning.

The meanings of words are determined in two ways: by their dictionary definition or, in the case of a different language, by the use of a lexicon; and, more importantly, by their usage. In word studies, as A. B. Davidson said, the concordance is more important than the lexicon. How words are used by any given writer is the chief guide to what they mean for him.

For example, the characteristic New Testament word for "sin" is *hamartia*, defined in the lexicon simply as "missing the mark." But the lexicon gives no clue as to whether the mark is missed through weakness, poor but well-intentioned aim, or because the archer shoots at the wrong target. It is only when we look at the way Jesus, Paul, and John use the term that we see the meaning of "sin" as "willful violation of a known law of God": "Whosoever committeth sin is the servant of sin ... If the Son therefore shall make you free, ye shall be free indeed" (Jesus in John 8:34, 36); "Now being made free from sin, ... ye have your fruit unto holiness" (Rom. 6:18, 22); and "He that committeth sin is of the devil. ... Whosoever is born of God doth not commit sin" (1 John 3:8–9).

4. *Take the content of the passage as a whole and relate the key words to their context.* Try to read the passage as if you were reading it for the first time. Consider its relation to what has preceded and to what follows.

The principle rule of exegesis is "context." A text without a context may be worse than a "pretext." It may be actually misleading. How often 1 John 1:8, "If we say that we have no sin, we deceive ourselves, and the truth is not in us" has been waved as a club against the doctrine of holiness, quite oblivious to the context in which both verses 7 and 9 affirm cleansing "from all sin" and "all unrighteousness." The deception is not of those who humbly confess the cleansing blood of Christ, but of those who allege that they have no sin from which they need to be cleansed.

Context is of two kinds: literary and historical. The literary context is the paragraph, the chapter, the book, the Testament, and ultimately the whole of the Scriptures.

It includes the literary *genre* of which we have already spoken.

The historical context requires us to ask what these words would have meant to the persons to whom they were originally written, as far as it is possible for us to find that out. The literal meaning of sentences is their normal, customary sense in their historical context. While "all scripture is given" for us, "all scripture" was initially given *to* a specific person or persons. It is always helpful to ask, "Why was this particular event or idea chosen for inclusion in this context?"

This means that cultural conditioning must be considered. "Rightly dividing the word of truth" (2 Tim. 2:15) includes discrimination at this point. Paul's comments concerning marriage and about slavery in 1 Corinthians 7, and his requirement that Christian women wear veils and keep silence in church in 1 Corinthians 11 and 14, are examples of such cultural conditioning.

5. *Interpret each passage in the light of progressive revelation.* Especially must we be careful about reading back into the Old Testament the religious experiences and ethics of the New Testament, expecting of Old Testament personalities what is proper only in the New Testament age.

Where a statement appears in the Bible determines its theological weight and, to some extent at least, its very meaning. "Sanctify" does not mean the same in Josh. 3:5 ("Sanctify yourselves: for tomorrow the Lord will do wonders among you") as it does in John 17:17 (the high-priestly prayer of Jesus, "Sanctify them through thy truth: thy word is truth"); and it is only confusion to read it as if it does. By no stretch of the imagination may the speculation of Eccles. 3:19, "For that which befalleth the sons of men befalleth beasts; even one thing befalleth them: as the one dieth, so dieth the other; yea, they have all one breath; so that a man hath no preeminence above a beast," be taken to cancel the clear meaning of Paul's words in 2 Cor. 5:1–8 and Phil. 1:21–24 that death ushers the believer immediately into the presence of Christ.

This is not to deny the unity of the Scriptures. But the core of the unity of the Scriptures is Christ. The "center of gravity" in the Bible is the New Testament, and the heart of the New Testament is Christ.

When this principle is rightly observed, what is historically called "the analogy of faith" comes into play. The whole of the Scriptures interprets the parts of the Scriptures. No part of the Scriptures may be interpreted in such a manner as to distort the whole. Here is the difference between mainstream Christianity and the multitude of sects that have grown up on its margins. The sects are based, almost without exception, on their one-sided, special pleading emphasis on one aspect of the Scriptures to the neglect of the whole. What we must always seek is the "general norm of the Word of God."

This involves a measure of circularity, to be sure. The whole is known only through the study of the parts; and the parts, in turn, are only fully understood in light of the whole. Herein is the value of biblical theology for the student of the Scriptures. It offers the overview and the balance necessary to move easily from part to whole and from whole to part.

After the labor of exegesis comes the toil of homiletics. This is the task of organizing, outlining, illustrating, and carefully planning introduction, application, and conclusion. Whether the final work be done by writing in full, preparing a brief, or drawing up a short outline, it must be done. It isn't enough to gather the food; it must be prepared and "put on the table" in appetizing form.

Nobody who has ever done it denies that biblical preaching is hard work. But it's worth it, both for the immediate returns and for the long future.

Conclusion

Here is the challenge of biblical preaching in our day. Nothing can surpass its importance. Much is new in the work of the modern minister. Paul never ran a mimeograph or got out a midweek mailer. But preaching is as old as the Bible itself. In the pulpit, the pastor is in a true apostolic succession. He is doing the work of his Lord and the prophets and apostles of the Old and New Testaments.

Preaching is the "hardest, highest, and holiest" service possible to God and man; and there is no preaching more effective than biblical preaching.

To give of self, and not to count the cost,
To learn, to teach, to labor, and to pray,
To serve like Christ, the least, the last, the lost—
These were the beacon fires that lit the way.[3]

● **Mildred Bangs Wynkoop**

2

Responsible Biblical Interpretation

Extra blue ribbons should be awarded in heaven to those who have stuck faithfully with the uninteresting preacher through thick and thin. Of course, the boring preacher would have to finance and present the ribbons himself. God would not bother. He made His truth so interesting that whoever dulls it ought to have to be required to go into heaven's side door with his awards, if he gets in at all. The preacher's task is to preach the TRUTH—and do it interestingly.

Morton Enslin tells how he played the "Alphabet Game" through many a boring sermon.[1] He listened for words that began with each succeeding letter in the alphabet (no fair going to *g* until *f* came up). One virtue might be the rapt expression one would seem to wear as he listened intently for the next word with the proper letter. At any rate, a listener would be more sure of earning his blue ribbon by playing the Alphabet Game than by falling asleep in church.

An interesting sermon, as well as the true truth, is the least a preacher can contribute to the preaching event.

Truth is fabulously interesting. God saw to that. So if the preacher becomes "deadly dull," he has to really work hard to ruin that which has been handed to him so vibrant with life. And some preachers do work hard.

The Bible is our major Resource, but the fact alone does not solve the problem. An awesome responsibility rests on those who attempt to dig sermons from it.

A wholesomely shocking little book that keeps a prominent section of my desk warm is called *The Strange Silence of the Bible in the Church*, by James Smart. In speaking of today's problems, he said, "Sermons are rarely heard which open the scriptures to the community in such a way that the people themselves begin to be able to find their way between life situations and the [biblical] resources to illuminate life." And then Smart puts in the painful probe, "It is only our ineptitude that makes words dull which in their original utterance shook the community that heard them to the depths and endangered the lives of the speakers."

We are reminded of a little 5-foot-7-inch, white-wigged, 122-pound British preacher speaking from the Word of God to great crowds of people in the open fields. The spiritual force of his message was so powerful that strong men would literally faint during the sermon. John Wesley was a biblical preacher—and he was not dull to those who heard him in that day. Wesley preached holiness but not in a narrow, parochial sense. Holiness was to him a total Bible truth, a Church truth, that belonged in every corner of human life. It spoke to personal and social issues, labor problems, public education, cultural ideals, health and welfare matters. He preached the first of several sermons in his usual day at five o'clock in the morning, always to people who came knowing that he was going to preach. In a morally decadent day, England listened, trembled, and changed. And he preached from the same Bible we do.

To those who stand in the Wesleyan theological tradition, the proclamation of holiness becomes a virtual mandate. But when the more definitive term *scriptural holiness* is added, the whole question of responsible biblical preaching is encountered. All Christian traditions teach holiness. But quite frankly, the Wesleyan comes to his view from a different approach to his Bible and theology than others. Can we say what the Wesleyan approach is? The differences that divide the great theological traditions in Christendom lie here. Our task is not to argue the truth or error of the great traditions but to explore the primary assumption and methods underlying the activity of biblical interpretation and to so understand our own stance in theological matters.

Quite simply, Wesleyans assume that the Bible was given to communicate God's message to mankind. This communication was given in history, interpreted by "holy men," and preserved in written form to be understood by us. The retrieval of God's meaning in terms of our understanding is what interpretation is. But what is involved in the interpretation enterprise is not always obvious to those who engage in it. Two very different approaches are possible—proof-texting or induction.

Proof-texting

"Proof-texting" is one sure way to get out of the Bible what one wants to find there.

Basing the proof for the truth of a doctrine on selected sections of the Bible without regard for the context or the specific purpose of the author is proof-texting. In this approach the theological stance of the preacher determines what he will be able to find in the Bible. He is limited to those words or phrases that correspond to those he and his theological tradition use. Much of the Bible remains in a shadowy limbo because it does not speak to his point. Contexts, since they usually weaken the message he wants to declare, are neglected or even ignored.

Perhaps the most theologically dangerous spin-off of proof-texting is the tendency to actually misinterpret, even distort, a text of scripture, usually without malice aforethought, in order to assure certain theological results or denominational distinctives. (Don't look now, but the Calvinists tiptoeing behind you may not be the worst offenders. Wesleyans have been known to commit this indiscretion, too!)

As an example of the latter holiness proof-texting blunder, the following bit of conversation may be illuminative. "How often ought one to 'preach holiness'?" is a frequent question. There are two sorts of opposing responses, both of which arise out of a misunderstanding of what scriptural holiness preaching is. One says, "Don't overdo it. Preach once a month, or once a quarter, or once a year." The other says, "Preach it every time you go into the pulpit." And those who listen to him are apt to say, "We are tired of holiness. We wish our preacher would give us some food."

In both cases the problem lies in the fact that holiness is proof-texted and therefore interpreted too narrowly. It may mean a dry doctrinal sermon in which the bare theological bones are counted, or it may mean a constant exhortation to a certain experience with no life involvement indicated beyond it. Neither alternative is biblical preaching.

Induction

The opposite approach from proof-texting, namely, induction, asks the question, "What does the text actually say?" before it is dogmatic about what it means. Induction ranges out widely from the text into an exploration of the context, past the paragraph into the whole book in which the paragraph and sentence lie. Induction does not presume to know all the answers before asking the diagnostic questions and waiting for the answers from the context. Just as a doctor carefully explores all possible aspects of a patient's physical and psychological makeup to determine his diagnosis, so must a preacher discover all available information bearing on his text before prescribing remedies to fit the needs of the people.

The most basic diagnostic questions prove to be remarkably interesting. Who wrote the book? Who was he? What was on his mind when he wrote? To whom did he write? What was the point of what he wrote? How does the section in which the text lies relate to that point? What was the meaning of the text we are using to those to whom it was written? What is there about that meaning that speaks to the situation our audience is in? This type of honest interpretation will open the way for the people to learn to go to the Bible to find answers to their own questions about their own life problems when they are alone.

From such painstaking study arises a closer approximation to biblical preaching than proof-texting can ever approach. Messages come up out of the context with frequently surprising results. Floods of insight and revelation break over the dikes of fear and defensiveness to create new spiritual life and exciting creativity.

Hermeneutics—Responsible Interpretation ♦

"Christian preaching," says James Earl Massey," demands responsible hermeneutics. Simply stated, *hermeneutics* has to do with the task and art of interpretation."[2] Hermeneutics—a big word—means that interpretation is taken seriously and responsibly. Biblical meanings are discovered and expressed in contemporary idiom and made applicable to everyday situations. This task is a part of the package in which God's call is received.

A call to the Christian ministry is a call to responsibility in handling the Word of God. That Word must be interpreted, that is, properly understood and adapted to the understanding of those for whom it is intended. There can be no exceptions to this responsibility. The art of interpretation can and must be learned at whatever cost in time and concentration and strength and discipline it requires. No longer is the cop-out philosophy acceptable that gave comfort to the lazy preacher, "Open your mouth and the Lord will fill it."

Hermeneutics is a word coming from Greek mythology. Hermes was the god of language, who, it was said, invented language as a means of communication between the gods and men. From this mythological origin, hermeneutics comes to us with a useful background of meaning. Hermeneutics refers to the activity of communicating a message from someone (in our case, God's Word, in the form of the Bible) to someone (in our case, twentieth-century mankind). This communication requires that the interpreter be thoroughly acquainted with the Person and the meaning of that Someone as well as the "someones" who are to receive that message.

In a most absolute sense, the interpreter dare not substitute his own message for that of God, nor has he discharged his stewardship until that message is put into the form that the hearer can understand in his own situation. "God's Word in Man's Language" is the way Eugene Nida expressed it in a book by that title. Until missionaries achieve facility in a new language, they realize the imperative need to have an interpreter who can translate, not merely their words, but their ideas, their idiom, and the significance of what they are saying into the thought patterns of the people. The interpreter may need three or four times as long as the foreign speaker to get this across because some Western concepts are nearly untranslatable into a language which has no corresponding concepts. He learns that mere equivalence of word does not communicate anything. Communication takes more than a lexicon, it takes a life.

A discussion of responsible biblical interpretation falls naturally into three divisions: (1) *the preacher himself*; (2) *the Bible* from which the preacher derives his message; and (3) *the people* to whom he preaches. The first examines the problem of *eisegesis*, or that which the preacher brings with him to the preaching event; the second attempts to commend *exegesis*, or that which the preacher draws from his source; and the third leads into the *existential* dimension of the preaching event which is the ultimate purpose of the whole business. This purpose is that real, living, involved people must be brought into a personal encounter with Him who is Truth. Until the Word is put into human idiom, the preaching procedure is futile.

1. *The Preacher and Theological Biases*

Hermeneutics starts the moment the preacher closes his study door, because he himself is the first problem which is confronted in sermon building. The problem is called *eisegesis*, which means that the interpreter brings with him "notions, questions, interests and a definite mind-set" (Massey, p. 55), which predisposes him to certain ways of thinking. This affects his interpretation. Everyone has a bias which must be taken into account as does a compass which must be adjusted to certain geological and geographical locations to give an accurate reading.

31

Preaching is not done in an intellectually and spiritually antiseptic neutrality. All the preacher's heritage comes into that event with him. He has been stained by the prejudices, ideals, social attitudes, and theological emphases which have molded his mind. These colors are deep dyed. They did not wash off in the baptismal font. The preacher does not leave them outside his study door when he goes in to prepare his message.

These personal ways of thinking seem so natural that he without question assumes everyone accepts his point of view. A classic example is the Apostle Peter who so gloriously proclaimed the universal scope of the gospel on that first Christian Pentecost Day and the fact that Jesus of Nazareth would save whoever would believe on Him (Acts 2). But when it came to accepting Gentiles on an equal basis with Jews, he had trouble.

It is possible to go to the study as an uncriticized, white, male, American, holiness preacher, or an uncriticized Calvinist preacher, or an uncriticized black preacher, or an uncriticized feminist preacher—all touched by a bit of chauvinism. (Not all chauvinism is a white male disease!) To change our figure—we do wear colored glasses when we come to the Bible. These natural lenses can neutralize or even block some of the rays of light shining out from God's Word so that the truth which is seen is a partial truth and not quite accurately God's Word.

a. Self-criticism, Painful but Wholesome

There are those who say that it is impossible to escape some measure of bias. But objectivity is essential to truth, and it begins not in arguing yes and no over the interpretation of a passage of scripture. It begins, if it does begin, in the more responsible, rational activity which distin-

32

guishes men from animals. The human kind can take stock of his thinking and begin to ask questions about his heretofore undisturbed, unquestioned ideas—the ideas by which he judges the right and wrong, good and bad, true and false of all matters which come to his attention. Self-criticism is a noble art; it is the ability to look inward, critically, at oneself. It is the beginning of wisdom, the foundation of all learning.

Can we change our inner computer? Can one who has been taught that the earth is flat change his judgment-forming apparatus to accept a globe-shaped earth? Can one who believed that evil spirits cause disease become a respected and efficient scientist or physician who takes bacteria seriously? Can one who has held grossly faulty ideas of God learn about Jesus who corrects errors men have about God? Such corrections are possible, and the Bible proceeds on that assumption.

b. Some Values of Eisegesis

Eisegesis is the personal bias we bring with us to the Bible. It must be recognized for the danger that it is to biblical preaching. But Jay Williams in *Theology Today* suggest another dimension:

> As an interpreter of Scripture, each man brings with him a whole pile of intellectual and emotional baggage which cannot easily be dispensed with. In fact, to jettison it would be about like trying to perform a self-styled prefrontal lobotomy. In order to think at all, we must think with a cultural and linguistic context . . . which shapes what we see and what we are likely *not* to see.[3]

We must stop and ask: Is an empty, unbiased mind so desirable even if such were possible? All thinking requires a context of culture and language which not only hides some thing from us but discovers things to us few others would see. Besides the obvious projections of our heritage which bring some scriptural insights into focus, there is also a very personal and subjective preparation which sensitizes us to truth others miss. Deep sorrow, bitter disappointment and disillusionment, profound questioning and searching for meanings, loneliness, stabbing beauty, wonder and curiosity, inexpressible desire—any or all of these may serve to sensitize us to truths in the Word. They were always there but are freshly exposed and reserved for those whose souls have been bared by great emotion and experience to receive them. Less sensitive souls fail totally to "see" these truths. Extreme emotional and empathetic life experiences gave David a grasp of truth and faith which provides profound help to us in our extreme life experiences.

Bringing these highly personal sensitivities, peculiar dispositions, opennesses, and yearnings to God's Word, along with the ear that hears "the beat of another drummer," makes eisegesis not always a detriment to truth.

But eisegesis can be destructive of truth. The preacher must come to his task aware of his prejudicial "reading-into-ness" and humbly and prayerfully open himself to honest self-criticism. If he can recognize his blind, sometimes bigoted eisegesis, yet add his unique personal contributions to the "enlightenment" moment, a "happening" can happen, gloriously, to him and, in turn, those who hear his preaching.

A preacher does not, or should not, merely process truth, whipping it into palatable form to pour into other minds. He must first of all be possessed by it. He must become a living carrier of the truth. Deeply infected himself, he infects others in every contact. The religion of Jesus is more "a blessed contagion than a science. It is a divine infection that spreads from heart to heart. . . . When you have it you can't keep it."[4]

After we have been warned against eisegesis—seeing only what we want to see—and have recognized that a certain kind of eisegesis is necessary, we are ready to face into the truth that the Bible yields its dynamic to those who bare their soul to it. And baring souls requires a faith that we can trust our soul to God through the Bible. We can wrestle with it as Jacob wrestled with the Angel. Finally confessing his own nature, he received a new name to live up to. So can come to every truth-seeker a new dimension of understanding.

Leander Keck says it well:

> If there is not struggle with the text, no exposure to it, the text will degenerate into a useful tool with which the preacher hopes to sanctify ideas he already has. . . . Unless the word is *heard* it cannot be re-said. . . . Where there is authentic hearing, the preacher risks being vulnerable.[5]

So, in the final analysis, this Word of God is not presenting us with powerful passages to lift out and take up to hurl at others, thus slaying them with the truth. First of all that Word must slay us, compelling us to incarnate it. Only then can we use it to lead others to the Lord. Only then will they take orders from that Word for every detail of their own lives.

2. *Gold-mining the Bible—Exegesis*

The use the preacher makes of the Bible reveals his idea of what the Bible is for. If he perceives the Bible to be but a well of preaching texts for which he dips each time he preaches, his sermonizing will be disoriented and shallow. Hermeneutics is based on the conviction that the Bible is given, with all its diversity, as communication

35

from God to man. It is not a book of mystery and magic (even spiritual magic) but of revelation—an opening. It speaks to man's mind as well as to his heart. It must be understood before it can be obeyed.

The Wesleyan theological emphasis is built on this approach to the Scriptures. Not that Wesleyanism has a corner on this approach—far from it! But the typical Wesleyan doctrines arise from the assumption, derived from the appeals in the Bible, that God is revealing himself and that man is capable by God's grace of responding to that revelation. The view held about God and man and grace is the watershed between quite divergent understandings of theology. To the Wesleyan, the sweep of historical revelation is spoken to any and all men, not to any limited segment of mankind. On the basis of his observations, the Wesleyan feels that any limitations of that ability is imported from purely human assumptions about God and man. It does not come from what is disclosed by God about himself and humanity in the Bible.

The God whose nature is love has put himself into human history in order that mankind can understand what He is saying. Every new flash of insight is preceded by historical steps to bring the mind to the place where faith is possible. The master example is the coming of Jesus, which was heralded in innumerable ways. Its significance could not be shrouded in a cloud of mystery but was opened to the full experience of men: "That which we have heard . . . and seen with our eyes . . . and our hands have handled . . . declare we unto you" (1 John 1:1–3).

The biblical exegete, then, will need to trace these steps in order to explain Jesus Christ. The Book of Hebrews does this. The author comes up to Jesus through the Old Testament Tabernacle symbolism and the experiences in the Sinai wilderness. A Jew could thus understand Jesus as the Fulfillment of all the ritual. Stephen, in Acts 7, brought his snarling audience through the same history but selected another line of reasoning.

Every biblical truth has a history. Every Christian doctrine has deep roots. Every text has a context which draws the preacher into very specific human problems. The context is inspired, too, and cannot be divorced from the text if the sermon remains *the Word of God* not the empty *words of man*. Sermons cannot often bring all the historical roots into the pulpit, but these roots must keep the preacher tied to the Word.

The Bible was not given to us to read in bits and pieces such as a snippet or two pulled out of a "Promise Box" at the breakfast table. Many people have come up through a concept of the Bible which militates against a submission to the discipline of study. Some have thought that the Bible was a source of magic verses to be pulled out of the box to paste over our problems to make the pain go away. It has tended to make our religion a life of "snack-shop" consumption. Snacks are not only expensive but lacking in proteins and vitamins. The shallow biblical usages of today's pop religion cannot answer the real questions which our world raises. Getting hooked on religious slogans, chopped-off Bible verses, and serendipity sessions cannot, in the long haul, lead to spiritual health and sustained strength.

The Bible is not really the Word from God until it is used as it was intended to be read. "The Scripture," James Smart says, "was a Public Book for the church." Paul's letters, for instance, had to do with "what it means to be a church." They were written to the Christian community, calling it to its redemptive mission. "The Bible is marching orders for an army, not bedtime reading to help one sleep more soundly."[6] Which is quicker (we sometimes ask ourselves): a couple of "begats" or a couple of aspirins to "make me drowsy so I can get to sleep"?

Really hearing the Word allays unwholesome fears in order to drive us to courageous action. Every renewal of the church, Leander Keck reminds us, results from a new hearing of the Bible, listening for and listening to that "strange, disturbing, yet gracious word." This will turn the church outward to the world and away from its preoccupation with itself and its own image. A most unlikely but memorable title of an article in *Christian Century* says brusquely what we are trying to say: "How I Have Been Snagged by the Seat of My Pants While Reading the Bible." Author Walter Wink writes about the startling new vistas of relevant biblical truth that had transformed his thinking.[6]

Exegesis is listening intently to what the Bible has to say to the preacher before he says it to the people. But "listening to" is sweaty work. John Wesley speaks to this point in a hard-hitting address to the preachers working under him:

> How much shall I suffer in my usefulness, if I have wasted opportunities ... and droned away precious hours ... if I have loitered away the time in which I might have become acquainted with the treasuries of sacred knowledge. ... Have I used all possible diligence to receive the most accurate knowledge of the English Scripture? ... Have I ... attained a thorough knowledge of the sacred text ... of its literal and spiritual meaning? Otherwise, how can I attempt to instruct others therein? Without this, I am a blind guide indeed. I am absolutely incapable of teaching my flock what I have never learned myself; no more fit to lead souls to God, than I am to govern the world.[7]

"Listening to" involves developing an appreciation

for the Bible as literature. The wealth of literary forms must be interpreted according to its own genre. *History* must be read for what it is, not as theology. A theology of the Holy Spirit cannot be derived from Acts, which was intended only to tell us what happened and to indicate why it happened. Poetry like "The hills skipped like rams, and the little hills like lambs" is not scientific fact, though it portrays otherwise inexpressible truths. *Parables* point to one thing and should not be made to run around "on all fours" to flesh out a sermon from them. *Phenomenal* truth and *proverbial* truth must be carefully distinguished for what they are.

C. Peter Wagner summarizes the ideas in these words:

> Not all parts of Scripture were meant to serve the same function.... We should never go first to non-theological portions of Scripture to form any Christian doctrine or practice, then try to make the theological portions fit in. That is allowing the tail to wag the dog.[8]

Long and diligent and honest and deep study of a biblical book, or series of books, will eventually be rewarded by a grasp of the underlying relationship of the parts. When these previously unrelated parts mesh, the intellectual joy and spiritual rejuvenation and preaching power is almost overwhelming.

3. *The People—The Existential Dimension*

A young businesswoman was caught up in a very high spiritual "happening" in a recent Sunday morning service. Later she said, "But I cannot bring this into my Monday work experience. These are two worlds that won't come together." Why not? For the preacher, the goal of the interpretation of the Bible is to bring the two worlds together for the people to whom he ministers. Jesus' word to Peter is very apropos: "Feed my sheep." This is what hermeneutics is all about. The subject matter of the text in its concreteness must be stated in such a way that people can grasp it and learn to find in the Bible a word spoken to their specific lives.

This involves the preacher in knowing his people inside out. As a rule, unless the preacher makes himself available, the people tend to hide from him their real, secular problems. They may listen to the pulpit language with toleration but without grasp. Theological language becomes a set of labels with very little understanding of the content of the package they are on. Bible stories often remain simply fantasy—pious but not real. The whole of the scientific world is checked at the church door and left outside.

The moral dilemma of the modern world presses in on every side. Concerns such as the children's social problems, family planning, and abortion are simply on a different wavelength from that which the preacher speaks about. Personal problems of depression, fear, excessive desire, spiritual malaise, emotional insecurity do not seem to find answers in church. Too often the perplexed preacher, possibly troubled by the same problems, proposes too simple an answer to a complex situation: "You need another work of grace," or, "Jesus is the Answer," or, "Trust God more." These admonitions sound religious but they are hollow.

Often in preacher's retreats or workshops, the speakers grapple with these issues honestly and creatively. Most of the workshop participants are helped and agree. But, most will say, "All this is true, but I could not say these things from the pulpit. The people are not ready. They could not stand it." Morton Enslin, already quoted, says with great relevance, "The people were ready, and they still are. Frank, honest, and understandable insights into the preacher's thinking—certainties and uncertainties—are always welcome."[9] The people are needing to hear what the preacher is experiencing and what he is finding in the Bible which speaks to him.

Remembering that interpretation is for communication, the question needs to be constantly raised, "Are we getting the message through?" C. S. Lewis once said that in his opinion every ministerial student, before being granted a degree, should have to take an especially important and difficult theological chapter and translate it into language the ordinary layman could understand. Lewis was not primarily a theologian, but he had so mastered the field that he could speak to a growing radio audience on doctrinal matters and be listened to avidly. We today read what he said with increasing interest. What he said was simple but with enormous depth because it touched life.

The New Testament, so hard for us to understand now, was not difficult when it was written. Koine Greek was the common language of the people. It was not the King James classic language of that day but much more like the *Living Bible* type of talk. And the earthy, human Hebrew language of the Old Testament was the dictionary which gave meaning to the New Testament ideas. The sublime themes of the Bible, so often locked in technical language today, were originally conveyed in the language of the common man.

Much of black preaching today has anticipated and outstripped the contemporary hermeneutical concepts. Henry H. Mitchell, in *Black Preaching*, quotes Gerhard Ebeling:

> The Word of God must be left free to assert itself
> in an unflinching critical manner against distortions

41

and fixations. But... theology and preaching should be free to make a translation into whatever language is required at the moment and to refuse to be satisfied with correct, archaising repetition of "pre-doctrine."[10]

Mitchell says the black preacher has known this all along, and he shows us concretely how this is so. This could well become a pattern for all Christian preaching. We are reminded of two principles of the new hermeneutic which can contribute to our effectiveness.

a. The gospel must be declared in the language and culture of the people—the vernacular. People listen with unabashed eagerness to a gospel proclamation in the language and idiom they live with every day.

b. The gospel must speak to the contemporary man and his needs. The Sunday sermon must have something to say to Monday's labor problems. The sermon will not change the Monday world, but it can bring light to bear on it which will help the people to live with Monday redemptively. Sunday can be carried into Monday to make a difference.

Maybe the white, Western style of preaching has surrendered too much to a depersonalized gospel drained of the deeply human, realistic, earthy idiom the gospel came to us in. Maybe there has yawned between the pulpit and the pew a gulf that becomes wider as time goes on and theological terms become more stereotyped and rigid.

The alternative to the preaching that has lost its grip is not to resort to gimmicky, shallow, storytelling binges designed to compete with popular TV entertainment. The alternative is to become a Bible preacher—a very special sort of Bible preacher. Merely telling a Bible story with dramatic flourishes is not in itself Bible preaching.

The biblical preacher who interprets dynamically,

lives in the world of the Scriptures. "His most intimate companions are prophets, psalmists, apostles, evangelists with Jesus Christ at their center."[11] He must learn their language, listen to them, enter their world, hear what they have to say to him, and be shattered and then healed by them.

But more than that, he must be immersed in the world around him where his people work and live. Smart reminds us that these two worlds must begin to merge so that one speaks to the other. We must learn to look in the Bible and see past the cultural differences and recognize *today's* world there, not merely a strange, ancient, unreal world. Underneath the cultural overlay is the familiar world all of us live in.

A sermon that has become incarnated in a preacher who has paid the price of knowing his Bible—and knowing his people—can stand up to the challenge the people demand of it. The preacher can do something of what Jesus did, which was to open himself to the full view of people where they could see the sermon lived out. This is hermeneutics.

We cannot escape the force of the conclusion Henry Mitchell makes when he says, "'Hermeneutics' is a code word for putting the gospel on a tell-it-like-it-is, nitty-gritty basis."[12]

● **W. E. McCumber**

3

Preaching Great Paragraphs

An English pastor who was prejudiced against women preachers once said, "A woman preaching is like a dog walking on its hind legs; it's seldom done; and when it is done, it's poorly done." I do not share his prejudice. Let God call whomever He wishes to preach the Word! But the quoted complaint could be justly applied to much preaching from paragraphs of scripture—seldom done and poorly done. If this is true, why preach from paragraphs instead of phrases or verses? A few reasons are readily apparent.

Paragraph preaching is more *natural*. The Bible was written in paragraphs, not in isolated words or sentences. The basic "meaning chunk" (to borrow a phrase from Bernard Ramm) of scripture is the paragraph. Preaching from them, when done well, is bound to be more biblical and more biblically communicative. It allows the Bible to address its own message to the audience more easily than other kinds of preaching. The pastor who is compelled to

44

understand and explain a paragraph of scripture is less likely to use his text as a springboard for plunging into subjective ideas and interests. It is harder to free oneself from a paragraph than a sentence. The minister is called to be the servant of the Word, not to make it the servant of his own desires and opinions. Preaching is bound to the Bible, and a paragraph has more strength to bind than have isolated verses.

Paragraph preaching is more *helpful*. It compels the preacher, and trains the people, to use the Bible as it was written. Handling the Bible atomistically by seizing upon individual verses without regard to their context has exerted a baneful influence upon the church. Such proof-texting has buttressed every heresy. And it has allowed a misguided people to stamp as a "Bible preacher" someone who impresses the ignorant or uncaring by his ability to quote scores of random verses in support of notions which may be grossly unbiblical and subversive of genuine Christianity. The church deserves more honest and helpful preaching. Paragraph preaching is a powerful stimulus to a true handling of the Word.

Paragraph preaching is more *versatile*. It lends itself to a wide range of materials and helps the preacher to avoid monotony of theme. My mother once complained that a pastor changed his text every Sunday but never his sermon. If he had patiently and honestly examined the meaning of each text in its context and had preached from paragraphs instead of sentences, he would not have been trapped in a barren pulpit ministry. Pursuing one's way through a Gospel or an Epistle will force upon the attention of the preacher every great concept employed by evangelist or apostle to set forth the riches of Jesus Christ. Preaching from paragraphs doesn't make monotony impossible, but it does make it less likely.

Given such advantages, those who seek to do paragraph preaching must be concerned with three things: selecting the paragraph, expounding the paragraph, and doing this with variety.

1. Selection

The Bible furnishes an abundance of preaching material. We are embarrassed by our wealth, not our poverty, after a few years of study and preaching. The problem becomes one of selection. With so many texts crying out to be preached, what shall we choose? Several factors are involved.

a. The ability of the preacher. The pastor should know what he is talking about when he speaks from the pulpit. Some parts of the Scriptures are easier than others to exegete and expound. Until he has become adept at using the tools of exegesis and can unravel the knotty problems of the more difficult passages, a preacher is well advised to stick to simpler portions of the Scriptures. He should learn to walk before he tries to climb. But he should keep at the study of the Scriptures until he gains confidence enough to leave the lowlands and risk the mountains. He must not wait too long to pit his strength against some of the tougher parts of the Bible. As one has urged, "Wrestle with great themes even if they throw you." His rule should be to choose a paragraph he can handle.

b. The needs of the audience. The paragraph from which one preaches should have something significant to say to the hearers. Preaching is vastly more than supplying factual data or rehearsing ancient history. There are some paragraphs of the Scriptures that really do not speak to the felt needs of a modern congregation. As a sample:

46

The Levites: the sons of Jeshua and Kadmiel, of the sons of Hodaviah, seventy-four. The singers: the sons of Asaph, one hundred and twenty-eight. The sons of the gatekeepers: the sons of Shallum, the sons of Ater, the sons of Akkub, the sons of Hatita, and the sons of Shobai, in all one hundred and thirty-nine (*Ezra 2:40–42*).

Surely a man may avoid preaching from that paragraph all his life without feeling that he has cheated the people. Some portions of the Scriptures that may be of interest to the archivist or historian do not meaningfully address "the butcher, the baker, and the candlestick maker."

c. The sequence in a series of messages. If one is preaching through a book of the Bible, the process of selection is almost automatic. One simply goes on to the next paragraph or paragraphs that supplies the next unit of thought. Even so, the preacher may not choose to expound every paragraph of the book. Just now I am preaching through the Gospel of Luke, but I am omitting most of the teaching passages in the early chapters, for I intend to cover these in a future series from Matthew. Planning a whole series in advance greatly facilitates selection.

d. The suggestions of the people. Pastors sometimes poll the congregation for sermon suggestions. They can then compile lists of those topics, or chapters, or doctrines, or ethical issues the people would like to have treated from the pulpit. The minister is called to proclaim what people *need* to hear, not what they *want* to hear, of course. Most of the time people will respond from the level of needs—from what is "bugging" them. The pastor reserves the right to amend the list. Conceivably, a segregated congregation in an area of racial turmoil will not want to hear a sermon based on the parable of the Good Samaritan, but they need to.

e. The calendar of the church. The great days which commemorate God's mighty saving acts call for certain special materials. Other specific types of passages may be used to lead up to, and to lead away from, the sermons for these days. A series of paragraphs drawn from the prophets, relating to the coming Messiah, may well precede the Christmas sermon, while another series chosen from the ministry of Jesus supplies a rich foreground for the sermons on Good Friday and Easter.

f. The guidance of the Holy Spirit. This is a constant factor among the variables of selection. Every true minister desires this above all. He needs to remember that His guidance is not given magically. It need not await the hour for preaching. He is wiser to assume that He who spans all time and knows all hearts will guide the process of selection well in advance. Ted Martin's dictum about an order of service fits here too: "The Holy Spirit would rather interrupt a program than invade a vacuum." The Holy Spirit knows best the Bible's meaning, the people's lives, and the preacher's abilities. He can be trusted to supervise the paragraph selection of the prayerful and trusting pastor.

2. Exposition

Here the task may be discussed under the headings of understanding the material, structuring the sermon, and translating the message.

a. Understanding the material. This is the task of exegesis. Since interpretation of the Bible is discussed elsewhere in this book, it need not be enlarged upon here. If only for emphasis, however, let me say here that adequate tools for exegesis are available to any pastor— books that will help him to interpret the Book. These can be purchased for less money than ministers often spend

48

on equipment for hunting, fishing, and golfing. There is no justification for empty bookshelves and consequent shallow preaching.

Understanding demands that the preacher study the text in context, which includes (1) the paragraphs surrounding the one from which he intends to preach, (2) the entire book from which it has been selected, and (3) the whole tenor of the Bible with regard to the themes it contains. Word studies and theological motifs are important here, and so is the cultivation of historical imagination which projects one into the passage and its milieu.

As he studies the paragraph he should keep raising three questions: (1) What does it say? He must deal intelligently with any textual problems the paragraph contains. (2) What does it mean? The meaning is to be exported from it, not imported into it. What is the writer, himself, intending to teach by what he has penned? (3) What does it demand? Unless the text makes some kind of demand upon him, unless it summons him to some kind of response, he is wasting time to preach it. The minister traffics in truth for life's sake. "These are written . . . that you may have life." How does the truth of the paragraph apply to the lives of preacher and people?

b. Structuring the sermon. It is important that the ideas be preached logically, coherently, and progressively, for the human mind is created to respond best to such presentation.

A *point of focus* needs to be found in the paragraph. For example, in a message from Luke 7:1–10 the point of focus was the words "Jesus marveled at him." Why would Jesus marvel at this man? (1) *His love was unusual.* He was a Gentile who loved the Jews (v. 5). He was a master who loved his slave (vv. 1–2). This was rare in Jesus' day. (2) *His humility was unusual.* He thought less of himself

49

than others thought of him. They said, "He is worthy," but he said, "I am not worthy" (vv. 4, 6). This was not false modesty, for he knew himself to be a person of authority (v. 8). (3) *His faith was unusual.* Just as his soldiers carried out his commands, because he represented the Roman emperor, he believed that Jesus could command illness because he represented the kingdom of God. Jesus had not found such faith "even in Israel" (vv. 7–10). The entire sermon was designed to raise the challenge: Does Jesus find such faith, humility, and love in us?

This leads us to another thought. *The purpose of the sermon* determines its structure. Usually the purpose of the sermon will be that of the paragraph; the writer's purpose determines the preacher's. Sometimes he may need to develop a secondary theme, without, of course, contradicting the primary theme of the passage.

For example, a message for pastors was structured from the material in Acts 18:5–17. The purpose of the sermon was to encourage pastors to determine both the tenure and content of their ministries by no other consideration than the will of God. Paul was model of this attitude. The focus was on verse 11: "And he stayed a year and six months, teaching the word of God among them" (RSV). The structure:

(1) *The Jews couldn't run him off.* They "opposed and reviled him" (v. 6). They launched "a united attack" upon him (v. 12). Despite the opposition he stayed at his post, for God ordered him to remain (vv. 9–10).

(2) *The church couldn't tie him down.* "He stayed a year and six months" and then moved on under marching orders from the Spirit. When turmoil subsided and problems lessened, he might have comfortably "homesteaded" the church there. But neither his friends nor his successes

(vv. 7–8, 10) could dissuade him from the will of God for his ministry.

(3) *The devil couldn't shut him up.* While he stayed, he "was occupied with preaching" (v. 5) and with "teaching the word of God" (v. 11). When dragged before Gallio, though circumstances prevented him from speaking, he was ready and willing "to open his mouth" (v. 14). What a model of the dedicated and unintimidated minister! Neither troubles nor pleasures could silence his message or dictate his tenure. He went where he went, stayed where he stayed, and preached what he preached out of conviction that it was all the will of God for his ministry.

Luke's primary purpose in writing these paragraphs was to record a segment of Early Church history. A secondary purpose was to display the inoffensive nature of Christianity to Roman officialdom. Perhaps a tertiary purpose was to argue the validity of Paul's apostleship. Without contradicting any of these, the passage can be structured and preached for the purpose of challenging pastors to singleminded devotion to God's will for the time, place, and content of their ministries. The subtheme does not force the passage to say or mean anything foreign to itself.

In structuring the sermon, we must *limit our ideas* to achieve effectiveness. Many paragraphs are so rich in possibilities for preaching that one could use them all only by preaching a series of sermons from the same paragraph. To prevent rambling and to achieve cohesiveness, the pastor must be disciplined to reject all the ideas arising out of the passage that do not contribute to the purpose of the sermon.

John 2:1–11, which records Jesus' first miracle, is such a paragraph. The presence of Jesus at the wedding evokes a sermon idea on Jesus and our social life (vv. 1–2). The relationship of Mary to Jesus is intriguing; she fails as an intercessor (v. 3) but succeeds as an advisor (v. 5). The "six stone jars" standing empty speak of the failure of ritualism to give life (v. 6). The obedience of the servants in filling the jars "to the brim" reminds us that full obedience brings full blessing (v. 7). The good wine served last speaks of the increasing joy of the Christian life (vv. 9–10). Ideas are jumping in every direction as one reads this passage. A point of focus and a purpose for the message keeps us from a sermon that goes everywhere and ends nowhere.

I found that focus once in the phrase "beginning of miracles" in v. 11. The sermon was addressed to a church living in the past, mooning over the "good old days," and doing little about the present challenge. The purpose of the sermon was to help them see the past as promise, and to believe that God was as able and willing to work today and tomorrow as He had been yesterday. The introduction acknowledged that the conversion of water into wine was a tremendous incident, manifesting the glory of Jesus as the Son of God, and deepening the faith of the disciples. But it was just the beginning. Brief allusion was then made to the other six "signs" which John records: The healing of the officer's son, the healing of the paralytic, the feeding of the multitude, the walking on the sea, the healing of the man born blind, and the raising of Lazarus. Even these were not all. Many of Jesus' miracles were left unrecorded (20:20; 21:35). From this "beginning" a single proposition was deduced: *God's first miracle is never His last*. There will always be more to come. (1) Application was first made to the individual believer. Beyond the miracle of conversion God could provide miracles of cleansing, healing, feeding, and witnessing. (2) Application was then made to the corporate church. God's love

52

and power were only beginning in the foundation of the church. There could be and would be future miracles of revival, soul winning, and church growth. It was an effective blow at ancestor worship, but the strength of the blow lay in the concentration of ideas.

c. Translating the message. Exegetical accuracy and structural efficiency will not assure success in preaching if the preacher fails to speak the language of the people. His biblical and theological studies have involved language that is technical and not popular. He can easily forget that what is familiar to him is an unknown tongue to the congregation. Let me suggest three simple aids to communication.

(1) *Keep your sermon language simple.* Use theological terms only when you must, and then carefully define and explain them in words and by illustrations the hearers can grasp. Preaching over people's heads, as one Scotsman observed, does not argue superior ammunition but inferior shooting.

(2) *Bring the people into the study when preparing the sermon.* In imagination gather a cross section of the audience; and as you write, keep asking them, Is this clear? The issue is not whether it is clear to you, but whether it is clear to them.

(3) *Write for the ear, not for the eye.* Writing orally is crucial to the pastor's task. If people are reading, and meanings are missed or ideas are fuzzy, they have leisure to reread until things break clear. But when you preach, it is going by them one time only. They cannot stop to reconsider anything without missing what follows. Spoken prose must be plainer than written prose or communication bogs down. You will be speaking to the ear, so write for the ear when preparing to preach.

Variation

In paragraph preaching, as in all preaching, variety is desirable. The attention span and interest quotient of the average churchgoer is quite limited. Unvarying presentation of truth tends to further shrink the limits.

The available material is certainly varied. The Bible contains an intriguing variety of literary types, dealing with many kinds of truth, and reflecting in its pages the unique personalities of those who speak and write. You must learn to handle this material so that its pluralism of type, style, and teaching comes through to your people. The surest way to do this, in preaching from paragraphs, is to plan and preach constantly changing series of messages.

a. A book series. The novice should keep the series short, working through one of the briefer Epistles, such as Galatians. Two sermons may explore *the personal issue* in chapters 1 and 2. Two more sermons may expound *the doctrinal issue* in chapters 3 and 4. A final two can enforce *the practical issue* in chapters 5 and 6. When the pastor is ready for a longer series, he can preach consecutively through the Gospel of Mark or the Epistle to the Romans. Until the congregation is accustomed to, and appreciative of, series preaching, he should keep each series to a dozen or fewer sermons.

b. A doctrinal series. Obviously, a few sermons cannot provide a complete theology. But a good measure of basic truth can be expounded, and the appetite of the church will be whetted for more of the same at a later time.

In addition to a series which gives a sermon each to several doctrines, a series might explore the interrelatedness of a major doctrine to others. One such series which I found useful was centered around the doctrine of holiness

54

in human experience, with the sermon materials drawn from First Thessalonians:

(1) Election—The Origin of Holiness. 1:2–8.
(2) Conversion—The Entrance into Holiness. 1:9–10.
(3) Christian Perfection—The Essence of Holiness. 3:9–13.
(4) Entire Sanctification—The Completion of Holiness. 5:23–28.
(5) The Second Advent—The Consummation of Holiness. 4:13–18.

These sermons prompted a surprising number of requests for additional sermons elaborating other doctrines.

c. An ethical series. A topic in this area is sure to arouse interest and provoke response. People need to know what the Bible teaches concerning the moral issues at the forefront of controversy today. Because the Bible is a book about God and people and relationships, it touches upon all that is relevant to daily life in a real world. In such a series special caution must be taken to let the paragraph speak its own message and not to force it to speak the personal opinions of the preacher.

d. A chapter series. Sermons based on the great chapters of the Bible can be fruitful. Many psalms lend themselves to this kind of treatment, as do certain chapters in the Gospels and Epistles. One thinks immediately of Psalm 1, Psalm 130, Mark 5, Matthew 28, Luke 15, John 17, Romans 12, Hebrews 11, Revelation 20, and others. The value of such a series extends beyond the message of each chapter in itself. It awakens interest in the whole book from which the chapter is taken, and it encourages the people to do more individual reading and study of the Scriptures.

e. A topical series. Utilizing certain literary types, such a series can provide refreshing variety. Apparent examples are the parables and the miracles of Jesus. The seven "signs" in the Gospel of John supply choice material for sermons witnessing to the lordship and saviourhood of Jesus, leading up to the supreme reality to which the "signs" point—the Crucifixion and Resurrection. This would make a good pre-Easter series. The negative and destructive conclusions of certain form critics notwithstanding, the various forms of which the biblical materials are comprised furnish some captivating possibilities for series preaching.

f. A narrative series. The Old Testament stories and Acts offer choice options for such a series. Some of your people have known these stories since childhood, but to preach them in the light of their setting within the redemptive purpose of God will open new vistas of truth for the hoariest veteran of Sunday school instruction. A former parishioner once said, "Of all the messages you preached, I found those Sunday night sermons based on Old Testament stories the most memorable and helpful. Do you still preach sermons like those?" I do.

g. A character series. Singling out individuals from the Scriptures has rich possibilities. People enjoy hearing about people. These sermons will be based upon several paragraphs. Some of the material will be from passages the pastor will not read in the service, but all will be integrated by the units of revelation which he does read and expound. Here is such a series on "Yesterday's Men with Today's Message."

    (1) The Wise Man Who Played the Fool (Solomon)
    (2) The Preacher Who Resented Success (Jonah)

(3) The General Who Swallowed His Pride and
Tasted Salvation (Naaman)

(4) The King Who Kept His Word but Lost His Soul
(Herod)

(5) The Man Who Found Blessing in the Place of the
Curse (Bartimaeus)

(6) The Man Who Was Lifted Up by Looking Down
(The Publican)

(7) The Man with Good News Who Couldn't Tell It
(The Blind Man at Bethsaida)

(8) The Man Who Drifted to Ruin on the Currents of
Compromise (Demas)

(9) The Man Who Came in Through the Roof and
Went Out Through the Door (The Paralytic)

The possibilities of paragraph preaching in series
with invigorating variety are more than a lifelong ministry
can exhaust.

● Randal E. Denny

4

Preaching Great Bible Books

In the cartoon series "Peanuts," Lucy asks Charlie Brown, "What's the shortest verse in the Bible?"

When he couldn't answer, she commented, "You don't know very much about theology, do you?"

The man in the pew will be helped in his ability to relate faith to life by preachers who turn from isolated facts and details to the vast panorama of biblical truth. Alan M. Stibbs suggests the preacher who is "faithful can adequately discharge his stewardship only if he preaches the whole Bible and the Christ of all the Scriptures. He ought, therefore, to make it plain, by the comprehensive variety of his themes, that his textbook is the whole Bible."[1] In biblical study, one ought to use the microscope on a verse, but the wide view and broad horizons of the Scriptures must not be neglected. James Stewart put it well:

There are tens of thousands of people today who are quite unable, where the Bible is concerned, to see the wood for the trees. You will be doing no small service if, leading them to vantage-points above the lower levels, you show them the country spread out before them like a map, and the glory of the land of far-stretching distances.[2]

The preaching pastor will enrich his own vision and whet the appetite of his hearers by giving them a bird's-eye view of a whole Bible book or a series of sermons from a great book of the Bible. One pastor conquered midsummer Sunday night slump by preaching a series of single book sermons:

Job—"Why Must a Good Man Suffer?"
Psalms—"How to Enjoy These Songs"
Proverbs—"How a Young Man Should Live"
Ecclesiastes—"What Is Best in Life Today?"[3]

In selecting a whole book sermon, one needs to start by discovering what problems and issues confront the people. Avoid answering questions no one thinks of asking. The themes of the books of the Bible are meaningful for the man in society today. As William Barclay summarized,

The true preacher starts where his people are— even if he has to learn about things he never in his life heard about before. The sermon which is above a congregation's head is not a good sermon; it is a bad sermon. It is simply the sign of a marksman who cannot hit the target. Be it noted that the preacher does not wish to leave his people where they are—far from that. But he begins from where they are to lead them to where he would wish them to be.[4]

The Bible is the preacher's greatest tool in meeting men's needs. Harry Emerson Fosdick put it well: "The

59

Bible is a searchlight, not so much intended to be looked at as to be thrown upon a shadowed spot."[5] The study of the Bible is a postgraduate course in the richest library of experience. These 66 books are the Word of God's Power. J. B. Phillips wrote that while translating the New Testament, he "felt rather like an electrician rewiring an ancient house without being able to 'turn off the mains.' " The expositor who gets a hold on the message of the great books of the Bible becomes aware of the mighty, powerful message God has delivered for our twentieth-century world.

Single Sermons on Great Bible Books

The book sermon is probably the most difficult assignment for most preachers. The larger body of material makes the preparation more complex. One writer warns, "This sermon is admittedly difficult to come by, and it will come only after a complete immersion in the book itself. It comes at the end not at the beginning of a long study."[6] However, it is an exciting way to acquaint the congregation with the message and contents of the great books of the Bible. The long-range view is worth the climb.

A Library to Be Discovered

The man in the pew may see the Bible as a collection of lessons or texts, and the new Christian may view the Bible as a maze of undiscovered information. While the Bible is bound as one Book, it is a collection of books containing all kinds of material—biographies, laws, history, love songs, sermons, proverbs, hymnbook, and much more. Though written by physicians, prophets, shepherds, kings, historians, missionaries, and poets over a 1,500-year span, there is one underlying theme—man's relationship to God.

This library of spiritual truth, according to Donald G. Miller,

> is not marvelous for the number of its ideas, but for the infinite variety of ways in which it presents a few very great ideas. To reflect the Bible's own variety in successive sermons would, in most cases, be a more effective savior from monotony than the efforts of the preacher's own individuality.[7]

The purpose of preaching single book sermons is to expose this library to give clear understanding of each book's message for today. It must answer the question every sermon must undergo: "So what?" For example,

> [There are] many sermons that may be preached *about* Genesis, but we are here interested in the sermon *of* Genesis. This means cleaving to the cardinal idea of the book as clearly expressed in one declarative sentence. . . . The purpose is not to tell history but to use it as the means of revealing the need and the means of God's redemptive work in His created world.[8]

The preacher needs to be fair to the book, giving its message in its own proportions and divisions, not just his own "happy thoughts" on the book.

Keep to the Main Issues

Learning to be selective is the challenge of the expositor. The dean of American preaching, Andrew Blackwood, said,

> The secret of popular effectiveness is largely in omitting many things of interest and value in order to present the book as a whole from a single point of view. In other words, the aim is to preach a helpful, uplifting sermon, and not to dissect a part of the Bible in order to display the bones.[9]

61

Unlike a running commentary, the preacher must ruthlessly omit points irrelevant to the main theme. One should not put too many people and too many incidents in the single book sermon. Harold Knott wrote, "The only thing that determines the scope is, that the sermon must be a unit of thought and an orderly and complete working out of some propositions which gives the point on which the development is concentrated."[10]

Single book sermons can arouse the curiosity of the congregation to explore each book more thoroughly. It is done, however, by the preacher "reporting what is on the menu and by allowing his congregation to taste every dish, but he must not take time to count all the beans and every little slice of bread."[11]

Method of Development

Having written at least two books on single book sermon studies, Dwight Stevenson followed a four-stage development. Gleaned from his books is this suggested method of development:

STAGE ONE: *Review the Bible book by reading at least three versions.*

From one's own impressions, several questions need to be answered:

(1) What is the main theme of the book?
State it in one sentence.
Give it a modern-day title.
(2) Are there any significant subordinate themes?
Write down any special or peculiar emphases.
(3) How is the book organized?
Outline it in one's own words.
(4) What is your personal reaction to the book?
Write down one's own personal response.

STAGE TWO: *Begin research reading "Introductions" to books of the Bible and commentaries.*
Summarize the findings by comparing and contrasting points of view.
Answer the following questions:
(1) When was the book written?
(2) To whom was it written and what was the historical, sociological, and religious situation?
(3) Who wrote the book?
(4) For what purpose was it written?
(5) What is its main message?
(6) How is the book's message organized?

STAGE THREE: *Develop a catalogue of sermon starters which include the following information:*
(1) The scripture itself.
(2) The suggested topic.
(3) A brief paragraph as the beginnings of a proposition.
(4) The aim or purpose of the sermon; why is this sermon needed?
Each sermon starter should be at least 75 to 150 words in length in order to retain the basic ideas for later use.

STAGE FOUR: *The development of the book sermon to its final stage.*[12]

Having developed the outline, one would do well to remember that

Phillips Brooks once remarked that the way to avoid the boniness of a skeleton is not to get rid of the skeleton, but to put flesh on it. The way, therefore, to give a sermon life is not to get rid of its points, but to make them as clear as possible and then to clothe the structural elements with flesh.[13]

63

Variety of Presentation

The axiom is well heeded: "Variety is the spice of life." There are many ways to present truth. Here are four ways of using the single book sermon.

First, "The sermon may be built upon the general analysis of the entire book. The main sections constitute the heads of the sermon."[14] The essence of each section of the book is stated in terms that support the central message as each part strengthens the whole. Here is a classic example.

THEME: *The Running Prophet*

1. Running from God (Jonah 1)
2. Running to God (Jonah 2)
3. Running with God (Jonah 3)
4. Running ahead of God (Jonah 4)

Second, "Each book has a special purpose or central teaching. The purpose will furnish the theme, and the several passages in the book relating to the theme will constitute the main divisions of the message."[15]

A sermon text for the whole Gospel of John could be John 20:31, "But these are written, that ye might believe that Jesus is the Christ, the Son of God; and that believing ye might have life through his name." The segments and specific incidents throughout John's Gospel could point to the central theme stated in 20:31.

Since the broad sweep of First Thessalonians deals with Jesus' return, this treatment would give a meaningful interpretation and inspiration:

THEME: *The Second Advent of Christ*

1. The expectation of His coming (1:9–10)
2. The joy of His coming (2:19–20)
3. The prospect of His coming (3:11–13)

64

4. The events of His coming (4:13–18)
5. The time of His coming (5:1–7)

Third, "Another method is to state the spiritual lessons of the book."[16] The significant spiritual teachings might be a natural outline and development. For contrast and comparison, let Jonah be approached in a different presentation. The truths of the Book of Jonah can be listed and arranged as follows:

THEME: *The Spiritual Teaching of Jonah*

1. The universality of God's grace
2. The impossibility of escaping God and our mission
3. The grave consequences of disobedience to a child of God
4. The unreasonableness of some godly men

Bishop Westcott had a theme developed later by Robert Law of Edinburgh as a single sermon on First John:

THEME: *The Glory of Christian Fellowship*

1. Fellowship with God in light (chaps. 1–2)
2. Fellowship with God in love (chaps. 3–4)
3. Fellowship with God in victory (chap. 5)

Fourth, "The final method of book exposition is the Christocentric element in each book."[17] All the way from Genesis to Revelation is the scarlet thread of the person of Christ. Each book gives meaning to the place of Christ in God's great plan. Charles Wesley described his own ministry: "I stood up and offered them Christ."[18] The 66 books offer Jesus. An unknown author has written the following oft-quoted outline of the Bible:

> In Genesis, Jesus is the "seed of the woman" that bruises the serpent's head. In Exodus, He is the Paschal Lamb whose blood upon the lintels and the

65

doorposts caused the destroying angel to "pass over."
In Leviticus, He is the great High Priest whose inter-
cessions are accepted for all who believe. In Numbers, He is the guiding Pillar of Cloud and Fire on the
way to our promised land. In Deuteronomy, He is the
Prophet "like unto Moses" who shall teach his people
and guide them unerringly.

In Joshua, He is the Man with the drawn sword,
come to command the hosts of the Lord and to lead
them on to victory. He is the Judge just and supreme
in the Book of Judges. He is the model Husband in
the Book of Ruth. He is the unerring Seer in the Books
of Samuel, the faultless King in the Books of Kings,
the unfailing Sovereign in the Books of Chronicles,
the pattern Preacher in Ezra, the Restorer of the waste
places in Nehemiah, and the Deliverer of the nation
in the Book of Esther.

In Job, He is the Lord of the resurrection and the
Daysman or Umpire who will give us consideration in
the game of life. In the Psalms, He is the Good
Shepherd, the Shield and Buckler, the Fortress and
Strong Tower. He is the personification of Wisdom in
Proverbs and Ecclesiastes, and the ideal Lover in the
Song of Solomon.

In Isaiah, He is the Child born, the Son given, the
Prince of Peace, the wonderful Counselor, and
the Suffering Saviour. He is the Balm of Gilead and
the Great Physician of Jeremiah, the Only Hope of
Lamentations, the Reviver of the dry bones in the val-
ley in Ezekiel, the Stone cut out of the mountain
without hands which shall destroy all kingdoms of the
earth and itself fill all the earth in the Book of Daniel.

Then we come to the Minor Prophets, where we
find that Jesus is the Redeemer of the unworthy in
Hosea, the Outpourer of the full measure of the Spirit
in Joel, and the Giver of abundant harvests in Amos.
In Obadiah, He is the Enlarger of Israel's inheritance.
In Jonah, He is the merciful Ruler. In Micah, He is

the Gatherer of the nations to Zion. In Nahum, He is the Healer of Bruises. In Habbakkuk, He is the Inheritance that remains when the fig tree fails to blossom. He is the Author of Israel's song in Zephaniah, the Beautifier of the new Temple in Haggai, the Opener of the cleansing fountain in Zechariah, and the Purifier of the sons of Levi in Malachi.

In the New Testament, Jesus breaks forth as the Messiah of the Jews in Matthew, the peerless World Worker in Mark, the Son of Man in Luke, and the Son of God in John. He is the Outpourer of the Holy Spirit in Acts, the Author of the law of life in Romans, the Head of the Church in Corinthians, the Giver of free salvation in Galatians, the eternal Author of holiness in Ephesians, and the highest Goal of life and eternity in Philippians. He is the Indwelling Christ in Colossians, the Lord of the Second Advent in First and Second Thessalonians, the ideal Pastor in Timothy and Titus, and the Friend of the friendless in Philemon. In Hebrews, Jesus is the Antitype of all types; the Head of all creation, higher than angels, and yet lower than angels in that He tasted death for every man. His blood takes the place of all the blood of beasts and birds that ever died on Jewish altars, and through the rent veil of His smitten body He makes a way for us to enter into the inner sanctum—where God himself sits upon the throne of His glory. In James, Jesus is the Pattern for practical living. In Peter, Christ's is the voice of thunder. In John, Jesus is the personification of Love. In Jude, He is the God of lightning. In Revelation, Jesus is the Alpha and the Omega.

A young man starting out in the ministry sought advice from an aged pastor in London. The old man responded, "I will give you a piece of advice. In every town in England, no matter how small, though it be hidden in the folds of the mountains or wrapped round by the sea, you can find a road, which, if you follow it, will take you to

London. Just so, every text you choose to preach from will have a road that leads to Jesus. Be sure you find that road and follow it. Be careful not to miss it once!"

Ways to Use Single Book Sermons

One pastor gave one book sermon a month, thus finishing the Bible in 5½ years. Another minister used the book sermon as an introduction to a new series of sermons on an assigned book.

The writer began with Genesis, preaching from an entire book each week, and ending with Revelation. The result in biblical understanding and the marching view of biblical history was worth the effort. It put the preacher and layman on the zest of the hunt.

If one wishes to begin with the easier books in the New Testament for a taste of the excitement, these are the 15 easier books listed approximately in increasing difficulty: Philemon, 1 John, Philippians, Acts, James, 1 Thessalonians, 1 Corinthians, 1 Peter, 2 John, 3 John, Galatians, Mark, Matthew, Luke, and John.

The 12 most difficult books listed approximately in decreasing order of difficulty are: Hebrews, Revelation, Romans, Ephesians, Colossians, 2 Thessalonians, 2 Peter, Jude, 2 Timothy, 1 Timothy, Titus, and 2 Corinthians.

Series Sermons on Great Bible Books

The study plan of preaching through one of the great books of the Bible is one of the happiest, most fruitful preaching programs a man can share with his parishioners. Many of the principles of preparation, discovery, methods, and presentation are the same as discussed in the section of Single Sermons on Great Bible Books. However, the portions or divisions of the book are allowed to grow in more detail. There is a wonderful sense of progression as pastor and people move through a systematic study of a majestic Bible book.

Dr. F. B. Meyer enthusiastically endorsed

the consecutive treatment of some book or extended portion of Scripture on which the preacher has concentrated head and heart, brain and brawn, over which he has thought and wept and prayed until it has yielded up its inner secret, and the spirit of it has passed into his spirit. The highest point of sermon utterance . . . comes oftenest and easiest to a man who has lived, slept, walked and eaten in fellowship with a passage for the best part of a week.[19]

Alexander Maclaren faced the difficulty of deciding each week which passage of the many clamoring to be preached should be selected. He lost time and creative energy trying to make up his mind. "At last, because of his wife's insistence, Maclaren began preaching his way through one Bible book at a time, always with liberty to omit passages here and there. In time he became known as 'the prince of expositors.' "[20]

A Good Reason for Bringing a Bible to Church

All too often laymen bring Bibles to church but have no occasion to use them. Preaching from the great books of the Bible in a systematic study will encourage the worshippers to bring the Book, to follow along, to go home and dig more deeply.

W. A. Criswell, pastor of the historic First Baptist Church of Dallas, wrote in *Christianity Today* magazine:

For 18 years I preached through the Bible. I began at the first verse in Genesis and continued through the last verse in the Revelation. . . . God blessed the procedure more than I could ever have hoped. The response of the people was amazing to me. . . .

The result is a finished story. So many people began coming to God's house that after a while they could not be packed in, although the auditorium is one of the most spacious in America. We finally had to begin holding two morning services.... Our people began bringing their Bibles, reading their Bibles, studying their Bibles. They began witnessing to others as never before. More and more souls were saved. The spirit of revival and refreshment became the daily order in the house of the Lord. It was the greatest experience of my life.[21]

How to Divide a Book into Series Sermons

The selected Bible book may have very natural divisions of thought. Sometimes the logical divisions may include several chapters at a time or necessitate several sermons within a chapter, such as Matthew 5. Since the Psalms are like hymns or songs, each psalm generally follows one basic thought.

Treatment of the Beatitudes under the title of *"The Habit of Happiness"* or Henry Drummond's famous sermon, "The Greatest Thing in the World," a verse-by-verse exposition, gives variety with closer detail. Donald G. Miller makes a very important point:

Books... often have a unity which must be recognized if the individual parts are not to be robbed of their meaning. It is the initial task of the interpreter, therefore, to search for the purpose and plan of the whole book before coming to grips with its parts. Failure to do this is often fatal to true interpretation.[22]

The context of the book and passages help to determine natural divisions. The writer is contemplating an in-depth series on The Acts of the Apostles. Having read through Acts in several versions and observing divisions on the book, he found that the *New International Version*

(NIV) has approximately 70 headings or subtitles. These may serve as good guidelines for a lengthy series on Acts.

A previous study in The Epistle to the Hebrews was prepared section by section. The following series serves as an example:

Heb. 1:1–3—"God Hath Spoken"
Heb. 2:5–10—"But We See Jesus"
Heb. 2:1–4—"The Wrong Road of Neglect"
Heb. 2:11–18—"Christ's Relationship to Men"
Heb. 3:1–6—"Two Considerations"
Heb. 3:7–19—"The Sin of Indifference"
Heb. 4:1–11—"The Rest of Faith"
Heb. 4:12–13—"The Relevancy of God's Word"
Heb. 4:14–16—"Our Sympathetic High Priest"

Often a chapter-by-chapter approach brings out major themes and keeps the study moving. Interest can be stimulated by encouraging the congregation to read ahead each week and simple outlines given each Sunday on which notes can be taken. One series followed the chapters simply:

Philippians 1—"A Christian Is Characterized
   by Confidence"
Philippians 2—"A Christian Is Characterized
   by Christlikeness"
Philippians 3—"A Christian Is Characterized
   by Conquest"
Philippians 4—"A Christian Is Characterized
   by Contentment"

A series on the Epistle of James rolls up its sleeves and gets right into the workaday world. It is marketplace religion. The writer followed this chapter-by-chapter progression:

James 1—"The Adventure of Adversity"

71

James 2—"Living What You Believe"
James 3—"The Need for Wisdom in Our Speech"
James 4—"Happiness in Christian Living"
James 5—"With Eternity's Values in View"

Selective Treatment

Not every stone overturned needs to be used. Unessential details must be omitted when they do not lend themselves to the theme being developed. F. B. Meyer wrote:

> The preacher... must select the material which is suited to his subject and reject the rest.... If he en were producing a commentary, he would be bound to neglect nothing contained in the passage. But he is not doing this. He is preparing a sermon upon a given subject which he finds in the passage considered, and, in order to have a clear and emphatic presentation of the subject, he chooses that which is related to it.[23]

Some books are so long that the man who preaches would do better to use selected chapters that are highlights of the book. Some of the Major Prophets lend themselves to such selective treatment. Blackwood gives sound advice:

> In working your way through a Bible book, if you come to a passage in which you can see no vision to share with lay friends, do not preach from that passage until you have seen your vision and felt your heart burn. Learn to select and to omit. If at present any group of sound words does not yield a message to uplift others, why attempt to pound out a sermon?[24]

Look for practical value that can help the listeners. Many scriptures can be discussed in a class situation that do not necessarily carry the proclamation of healing for broken hearts and of worship for the weary and spiritually hungry. Congregations eagerly await the message from the pulpit that can bring an explanation, an interpretation, and an application of the Bible to daily life. In his characteristic crisp style, Donald G. Miller wrote: "A sermon should be a bullet, not bird shot. It ought to be designed to hit the hearer in one vital spot, rather than to spray him with scattered theological ideas unrelated to each other which touch him mildly in a dozen places."[25]

An Antidote to Negative Preaching

Frightened and fearful preachers look for texts and subjects that bolster or condemn their own weaknesses. Left to a weekly search for something to say, one's own originality narrows the menu. However, preaching from the great books of the Bible in systematic series gives both preacher and his flock the balanced diet of the full scope of the Scriptures. The themes and emphases of the Bible are shared in the same proportion as God gave them through His Holy Word. God did not spend all the pages of the Scriptures in denunciation and condemnation. He filled book after book with the introduction of the world's greatest Joy—Good News for our day, too!

When E. V. Rieu began making a translation of the Bible for Penguin Books, his son remarked: "It will be very interesting to see what Father makes of the Gospels. It will be more interesting still to see what the Gospels make of Father."

After the completion of the translation, Rieu commented: "My work changed me."

Yes, the Bible is a powerful Book, and preaching great biblical books is a mighty work!

● Ross W. Hayslip

5

Preaching Great Bible Characters

Biography, wherever we find it, makes thrilling reading. And the Bible uses these natural interests as a channel for getting truth to us. There's nothing more interesting than people.

Thomas Carlyle correctly suggests, "The highest being reveals himself in man." That is why the Bible is filled with biographical material. Its pages are crowded with true-to-life people—men, women, children, kings, queens, commoners, soldiers, fishermen, tax collectors, priests, and shepherds. Some of them are known by their names, others by what they did. Stalwarts like Abraham, Moses, Joseph, and Paul have great details given about them. In other accounts there are only brief flashes, like the references to Pilate's wife, who sought to warn her husband; Simon of Cyrene, who became immortal as a crossbearer; Cleopas, who appeared on the Emmaus road;

and Eutychus, who fell asleep during Paul's preaching. Since people, not abstract propositions, are the aim of vital Christianity, we should not be surprised that the Bible devotes large spaces to biographies.

The Incarnation—the Word becoming flesh and dwelling among us—provides the noblest example of God's way of clothing majestic truth with human personality to make it understandable to common folks in every generation. Like secular history, the Bible teaches deep lessons through the lives of people. God illuminates His message by allowing us to see it in human form. So as we allow the personalities of the Bible to march before our congregations, they see truth. To see truth and to act upon it—that is the goal of all preaching.

Human Interest—a Magnet to Truth

As you journey through the Bible, you are constantly bumping into people. Starting in Genesis you begin with "Adam the Original Man," "Eve the Grand Mother," "Cain the Killer," "Abel the Righteous," "Nimrod the Hunter," "Enoch, Who Defeated Death," "Noah the Boatbuilder," "Abraham the Pioneer," "Isaac the Well-Digger," "Esau the Hunter," "Jacob the Wrestler," "Judah the Ancestor of Christ," and "Joseph the Dreamer." What an interesting cast of characters make up the first book of the Bible! The designations here given to them could be changed if a different aspect of their character is to be emphasized. You might look at "Adam, in God's Image," "Eve, Who Listened to the Tempter," "Cain, Who Questioned God," "Abel, Whose Sacrifice Was Approved," "Enoch, Who Walked with God," "Noah, Who Preached of Righteousness," "Abraham, Who Believed God," "Isaac the Sacrifice," "Esau and Jacob, the Unidentical Twins," and "Joseph the Governor of Egypt."

Along with Eve there are some other women worthy of note in Genesis. We find "Sara, Who Laughed at God," "Rebekah, Who Went to the Well," "Rachel the Mother of Joseph," "Hagar the Handmaid," "Remember Lot's Wife," and "The Wife of Potiphar." If we read the background material in Genesis, we come up with some real facts of interest for preaching about these noted women.

With a good concordance you can classify your Bible characters. *"Famous Failures"* might be "Lot the Mayor of Sodom," "Samson the Weak Strong Man," "Saul the Big Little King," "Solomon the Foolish Wise Man," "Jonah the Willful Prophet," and "Demas the Deserter."

Another way of grouping characters could be *"Workers for God."* We could list "Caleb, Who Called for Mountains," "Elijah, Who Prayed," "Daniel, Who Stopped Lions' Mouths," "Joshua the Leader of Men," and "Barnabas the Great Giver." The *"Marys of the Bible"* could be listed for a sermon grouping as "Mary the Mother of Jesus," "Mary the Sister of Martha," "Mary Magdalene," and "Mary the Mother of Mark." These are only a few of many possibilities; the biographical treasures of the Bible are limitless.

Bible Characters Capture Attention

Everyone loves a good story. The late General Superintendent Dr. Hardy C. Powers frequently admonished pastors to wrap the truth in a story so people could never forget it. And he did it so well and so frequently that his human interest stories will always be remembered by those who heard him preach. The Bible does that too.

The Bible character sermon has wide appeal because it speaks quickly and directly to the life experiences of the average man. Samuel Johnson expressed a commonly held opinion, "The biographical part of literature is what I like the best." And a churchy paraphrase of Johnson describes the preference of many sermon listeners from the pew, "The best part of preaching is the grace of God at work in real people."

Bible Characters Provide Examples

Children imitate without apology; adults try to be more coy about it but they imitate too. Nearly everyone wants to be like his ideal person. So worthy models deeply influence the development of Christian character. When the twentieth-century preacher announces his topic, "Religion for the Contemporary Businessman," he has the attention of all his hearers who are in business. Where in all the Bible could he find more preaching material than from Joseph's business career? The Joseph sermon leads the preacher to virtues like honesty, integrity, and optimism. Where else could a preacher find so much interesting material which simply cries out to be preached?

Frank Caldwell summarizes, "It is primarily at the point of indirect imitation of ideal persons that the angle of biographical preaching attains its greatest significance."[1] Such real-life examples provide interesting, useful scriptural prods to effective present-day living.

Faults to Avoid

Biographical preaching consisting of a running commentary is as dull as dust. But a piece of life about a Bible personality with clear, sharp focus often provides the exact truth channel needed by the preacher. Blackwood illustrates a way biographical sermons can be used to preach doctrine:

For example, think about the Providence of God in the life of a busy man. Instead of arguing about the matter, or trying to prove it by logic, one may begin with Joseph. One points out that during his early trials and disappointments, as well as during his adventures in high government office, God was looking out for his servant and friend. This is exactly what Providence means, in so far as it concerns one man. According to the root idea of the word, Providence means that God is the Good Provider. He looks ahead and prepares the way for the man who trusts in him. This is what the scholars sometimes call the doctrine of Particular Providence.[2]

Thus for a sermon on a major character, the preacher does well to focus clearly on one truth as found in the experience of the Bible personality.

To make the biographical sermon effective, the preacher must recognize that the Bible is not simply an anthology of biographies. The details must be filled in from historical and geographical data from the context and reference works like the atlas or Bible history books. A vivid imagination always provides a plus for biographical preaching, but imagination must be applied only after a thorough study of the time, the culture, and the geography of the Bible character under consideration. Useful biographical preaching gives needed attention to the life situation of the person being discussed.

Biographical preaching impact is frequently blunted when the preacher overloads his narrative preaching with long explanations and forced conclusions. Baumann summarizes the idea, "Narrative sermons have implicit suggestive applications throughout the sermon and it is unnecessary to insult the listener by tacking them on."[3] When one preaches on biblical personalities, he does well to allow his characters to speak for themselves. This is done by description, interaction, and conversations from the actual biblical record.

Good structuring of biographical preaching generally requires the preacher to deal with a time sequence from the life of his character; for example, youth, middle life, and old age, or a specific event or series of events like pre-conversion and post-conversion. Delightful, moving holiness preaching can grow out of a sermon on a particular New Testament personality before and after Pentecost. Another structuring which always secures attention is a contrasting of two Bible characters, like Jacob and Esau, Paul and Barnabas, or Peter and John. Still another way of building the Bible character sermon is to trace the actual spiritual development of a person. Then the hearer can reasonably conclude there is hope for me—I can make it.

Biographical preaching must center on the possibilities of grace at work in human life. There are failures and sins in the lives of biblical characters which provide a legitimate basis for warning, but a totally negative message without the proclamation of God's willingness to make every person new is not the effective kind of biographical preaching. Rather our most powerful pulpit proclamation announces that our God is redemptively at work in the common clay of human nature. Louis Pasteur caught the value of biographical studies when he wrote, "From the lives of men whose passage is marked by a trace of durable light, let us piously gather up every word, every incident likely to make known the incentives of their great souls, for the education of posterity."[4] And that is a worthy goal for every sermon on a biblical character.

Biographical preaching must avoid too frequent emphasis on one character. J. Sidlow Baxter speaks of exhaustless biographical resources: "Again and again we turn back to the figures which move before us in its pages, and find new relevances, new significances, new applications to our own times and to our own lives."[5]

Getting the Idea for the Sermon

Halford Luccock once correctly said that a sermon, like a river, begins in the sky. The preacher is a proclaimer for God. What the minister declares must have behind it the authority of "Thus saith the Lord." I have found that often God speaks to me through the apparent spiritual needs of my people.

I have found that the sacred seasons of the Christian calendar are times that I need to preach on the great truths that surround Christmas, Easter, and Pentecost; and for this, Bible personalities often help me. For example, there are wonderful character studies in the Gospels surrounding the events of Christ's birth. Before you use them, you must ask yourself what precise message you wish to bear. What truth is to be proclaimed? The object of the sermon is of more importance than its subject. At Christmastime the purpose is to center the minds of your people on Christ's first coming, and yet you want to help them deepen their own devotional lives.

A few years ago I worked out the following Advent series. With Luke 2:1 as a text I preached on *"God Uses Caesar."* The skeleton outline was: (1) God Uses Men to Work Out His Purpose; (2) God Uses Time to Work Out His Purposes; and (3) God Uses Events to Work Out His Purposes. Luke 2:2 formed my text for "The Governor Who Missed It." The main points were: (1) The Governor Was Successful in the Secular; (2) God Was Seeking in the Spiritual; and (3) The Governor Was Lost in Self-interest. The sermon that I think I enjoyed the most of this series was "Anna the Liberated Woman," with Luke 2:36–39 as background. Here is how I put it together:

80

A. *The Constancy of Her Character*
1. Anna was a prophetess. Four women are mentioned in the Old Testament as being prophetesses: Miriam (Exod. 15:20); Deborah (Judg. 4:4); Huldah (2 Kings 22:14); The unnamed wife of Isaiah (Isa. 8:3).
2. She was the daughter of Phanuel—his name meant "The Face of God." No doubt his spiritual influence was important in her life. Often as is the father, so is the daughter.
3. She was of the tribe of Asher—A Bible dictionary tells us of the failures of the tribe of Asher. Anna did not allow the failures of her ancestry to limit her.

B. *The Depth of Her Devotion*
1. She was of advanced age. Life can grow grander as it grows longer. You don't have to grow old inside. There are numerous examples of this from literature both old and contemporary.
2. She had lived many years as a widow. She had tasted life's disappointments. God's concern for widows (a Bible textbook or concordance can help us here).
3. She attended the Temple. Church attendance was vital in her life. There is joy in going to the house of the Lord. In a study of "Great Churches of America" I found one common factor. There is something in their fellowship that makes people want to come to worship together.

C. *The Continuity of Her Communication*
1. She fasted and prayed night and day. Prayer is the lifting up of the heart, mind, and will toward God. Fasting intensifies the prayer.
2. Thanksgiving formed her spirit of prayer. There are at least three things for which we can always be thankful: The fact that we are God's children; His great plan of redemption for all men; and His bound-

less love for the world. Romans 8:28 will help us in our thanksgiving.

3. A life of testimony (v. 38). "She spoke of him to all them that looked for redemption in Jerusalem." Dr. J. B. Chapman said, "We all need the grace of God to live the common life in an uncommon manner." This is the greatest testimony we can give—"Living for Jesus a life that is true."

Easter and Pentecost also abound with human personalities that can be woven into series of sermons that will not only spotlight the meaning of the season but will also present practical truth to help in day-by-day living.

Blood, Sweat, and Tears

Sermons never come easy. The modern preacher has a background of training in basic disciplines of literary composition. He has innumerable sermon helps. He has at his disposal countless volumes with all the fruits of scholarship, research, and fact-finding. Yet in spite of all these benefits he must, in the words of Halford Luccock, "toil as a miner under a landslide." Authentic preaching comes only from intensive effort at preparation.

When I have found the direction in which I wish to go and have found a Bible character to lead me in that direction, then I must put the ideas together in a form that will get me there by the most direct path. When I was a young minister, I preached from 45 minutes to one hour. Now in my mature years 30 minutes is my absolute maximum. It takes a lot more time and work to prepare the 30-minute message than the hour monologue. Someone has explained the difference between the approach shots of the British golfers and those of the Americans. The British generally play for the green; the Americans play for the pin. In our preaching preparation we need to go for the pin.

We must put into our sermons the blood of our own Christian personality, the sweat of our all-out effort, and the tears of our compassion for people.

About 20 years ago I sought to build a sermon that would challenge and inspire my people. The idea occurred to me that I could construct it around the theme "Three Men Named Ananias." I started by reading the accounts of these men as I found them in the Word of God. All of these men are mentioned in the Book of Acts. Here is how it all finally came together.

THREE MEN NAMED ANANIAS

Text: Acts 23:2; 5:1; 9:10

Introduction: We are looking at three different men who had the same name. Note the differences in their characters. A man's name need not make or break him. He can grace or disgrace his name based on his relationship to his God and fellowmen.

A. *The Religionist* (Acts 23:1–5)
   1. He was a member of one of the leading organizations of his day (Judaism).
   2. He seems to have kept the ordinances of his faith (various laws and practices of Judaism common in that day).
   3. He was very sincere in his beliefs and in his reaction to the Apostle Paul. (Sincerity does not keep us from being wrong.)

B. *The Hypocrite* (Acts 5:1–11)
   1. He was selfish in keeping that which he knew he ought to have given.
   2. He was doubtless fearful in that he failed to trust God in doing what he knew he should.

3. He was a pretender to an action which he had failed to perform.

C. *The Soul Winner* (Acts 9:1–19)
   1. He was a disciple (Acts 9:10). The meaning of true discipleship.
   2. He was a man of vision (Acts 9:10). Without a vision the people perish.
   3. He was a man of obedience (Acts 9:17). Doing the will of God leaves us no time for disputing about His plans. Obedience is indeed the Christian's crown.

I read and reread the scriptural accounts of these men until I felt acquainted with all three of them. Even now I occasionally rework the original outline, change some of my illustrations, and preach it again before a new group. Perhaps sometime in the future I shall take my three friends named Ananias and treat each one separately in a sermon, thus making a series of three.

Unity Can Come from Diversity

Doctrine can be preached from biography. The first sermon that I ever heard Dr. Paul S. Rees deliver was at a great holiness convention. He spoke on the subject of "The Fullness of Barnabas," and his text was Acts 11:24, "For he was a good man and full of the Holy Ghost and of faith: and much people was added to the Lord." Carefully and skillfully Dr. Rees preached a dynamic sermon on the manner in which a human being may live the Spirit-filled life. The character of Barnabas is indeed a great springboard for preaching the experience of entire sanctification. Let's try to put it together and bring the theme of the unity of holiness out of the diversified aspects of a man's character.

84

A Good Man

Text: Acts 11:24

Introduction: Holiness is religious principle put into the motion of everyday life. It is the perfect love of God embodied in the character of human beings. We see the life of holiness here exemplified not in an apostle but in a lay worker.

A. *Barnabas the Excellent*
1. Goodspeed's translation here calls Barnabas an "excellent man." He was largehearted rather than large-headed. "Goodness" was God's appraisal here, not man's.
2. Filled with the Holy Spirit. Refer again to Acts 2:4 as to what happened at Pentecost. Holiness is the fullness of the Holy Spirit.
3. Full of faith. This was one of the results of being filled with the Spirit. (Read Hebrews 11 for illustrations.)

B. *Barnabas the Evangelist*
1. "Considerable numbers of people were brought in for the Lord" (Moffatt). A considerable number—the experience of holiness will bring church growth.
2. They were added to or brought in for the Lord. Not to personalities or organizations, but to God.
3. Barnabas was an example of untiring efforts in his labor for the Lord.

C. *Barnabas the Encourager*
1. He saw the grace of God. One of the blessings and benefits of the holy life is to see God's grace in operation in our world.
2. He was glad. He knew that men would be happier as they grew in the grace and knowledge of the Lord.

3. His exhortation. He encouraged the new Christians to stay true. "With purpose of heart" is a phrase that tells us how holiness will fix our hearts on God.

Filling in Details

We take all of the relevant facts that God's Word gives us, knowing that the biblical writers are presenting close-ups rather than panoramas. We can use restrained imagination to fill in some of the blank spots in order to present a picture that will adequately show the area of truth that we wish to share. We do no violence to the truth as we seek to see these characters as they really were. In fact, it has been well said that a preacher without imagination is like an observatory without a telescope.

An old preacher friend, now long departed, had a holiness sermon focused on the character of the Apostle Peter. His simple outline was: (1) Peter by the Fire (temptation in the court of the high priest); (2) Peter in the Fire (sanctification on the Day of Pentecost); (3) Peter on Fire (evangelization in Jerusalem). He used these points with great force to show how the power of the Holy Spirit affected the life of Simon Peter.

Don't Bend the Character to Fit the Plot

There is a temptation in biographical preaching to magnify the negative aspects of the character by making his faults loom disproportionately large. I have heard Nicodemus pilloried in many pulpits as a coward because he came to Jesus by night. Ananias the liar is a far more familiar figure than Ananias who prayed with Paul in Damascus. We are far more acquainted with Judas the traitor than the Judas to whose house on Straight Street Paul was led blinded. If you are going to preach a series on "The Bad People in the Bible," you will probably select such characters as Cain, Esau, Balaam, Saul, Jezebel, Pilate, and Judas. If you do so, be sure to show how they are reflections of our modern society and as such deserve our sympathy for their failures, since we know full well that we too are human and not beyond the possibility of duplicating their acts.

I have heard some rather startling conclusions drawn about eternal punishment from the story of the Rich Man in Hell as recorded in Luke 16. Be sure that you do your homework when you prepare your message on this character.

If you are going to preach about James, be sure that you keep separate James, the son of Zebedee; James, the son of Alpheus; and James, the brother of the Lord. The James on the Mount of Transfiguration and the James who wrote the Epistle are evidently not one and the same, so they should not be identified as one person.

Variety Can Be the Spice of the Sermon

Sometimes the message can come through by the treatment of three distinct personalities.

INVESTING IN ETERNITY

Text: Matt. 26:13. *Scripture Lesson:* Matt. 26:6–13.

Introduction: Here is a study of three persons who had intimate contact with Jesus. Their response to the encounter was varied. Let us examine with care each person's response to the presence of the Lord.

A. *Simon, Who Did His Duty*
   1. Simon the leper is said to be a relative of Lazarus whom Jesus raised from the dead. He was cured of

leprosy or else he could not have mingled publicly with people. He could have been the leper healed in Matt. 8:2–4.

2. He had opened his home in hospitality to Jesus. The presence of Jesus makes a great difference in our homes. He comes only by our invitation and stays only at our desire.

3. When He is in our presence, we must decide what our relationship to Him shall be. Will he be our Saviour? Will we acknowledge Him as our Lord and Master? Shall we, like Simon, simply treat Him as a guest?

B. *The Disciples, Who Misread Motives*

1. They expressed indignation. Jesus was many times an embarrassment to His disciples. (e.g., the woman at the well at Sychar). The woman was a poet at heart while the disciples were prosaic. They made the mistake of criticizing another person's act of sincere devotion to God.

2. It was a waste to them. They said that it could have been sold. We can never sell the sacred. The amount that was involved was equal to a year's wages for a workman. We can never count any effort for God's service as waste.

3. "The poor ye have always." What Jesus was saying was, "If you love Me sincerely, you will give proper care to the poor." We can love and serve Jesus and also minister to the poor. The deeper we love Him, the more we will care for them.

C. *The Woman, Who Invested in Eternity*

1. She brought encouragement to Jesus in an hour of need. He was entering into the shadows of the Cross. She sought to encourage the Saviour.

2. She demonstrated devotion at its finest. We show our devotion quite clearly by our acts of worship. Kierkegaard said, "God has only one passion—to love and be loved. God is that which demands absolute love."

3. She made an eternal impact. Now nearly 2,000 years after this event we are drawing blessing and benefit from this simple deed of love performed by an insignificant woman. Our impact on life will be rated by what we gave to it rather than what we kept from it.

Conclusion: The story of this act is a story of three people whose lives were touched by the presence of Jesus. We remember two of these unfavorably, but the one whose service was motivated by love will forever be an example to us.

Find Yourself in the Bible

It is interesting to note that James comments on Elijah by saying that he was "a man subject to like passions as we are" (5:17). One great translator has put it: "Elijah was only a man like ourselves." When you see yourself in the Bible and realize that people haven't changed since the days when they appeared in Bible history, then it becomes easy to identify with people with whom you can share fears, hopes, and ambitions. The better you know a character, the closer you identify with him, the easier it will be for you to weave him into the message that you seek to proclaim. You are, in a sense, re-creating these personalities so that they are seen as real human beings. You seek to understand and interpret their spiritual experiences, their faith, and their relationship with God. As their re-creator, you owe them the acquaintanceship that can only come from a careful study of their lives.

89

Biographical Preaching Has Its Own Reward

Perhaps the greatest value of biographical preaching is that it gives you an opportunity to vividly show how the transforming grace of God performs miracles in human personality. This kind of preaching points out the possibilities of sainthood in every Magdalene; a rock of fidelity and firmness potentially in every impulsive and vacillating Peter; a guileless Israelite in the man who asks, "Can any good thing come out of Nazareth?"; an apostle of love in the young man who seeks authority and encouragement to invoke the consuming fire of heaven upon the heads of his opposers.

I once heard Dr. Thor Hall of Duke Divinity School define preaching as tearing loose the biblical message from its historical setting and using it to confront contemporary situations. We really understand the story of the Good Samaritan when the Jericho road becomes Main Street in our hometown, and the priest and Levite are seen as our neighbors who live on either side of us. The prodigal son is seen in the thousands of runaway kids that throng to our cities. The rich fool has far more meaning for us when we locate him among some of our friends who have become enamored with the world of the material at the expense of their soul's welfare. The biblical characters live all around us. Let them speak for you in full dimension and color.

● **Millard Reed**

6

Preaching Great Bible Events

Most of us believe that Jesus' words "Do not worry beforehand about what you will say" (Mark 13:11, NEB) refer only to the time when we are "arrested and taken away." They don't refer to our regular preaching schedule! On the contrary, we worry a great deal beforehand about what we will say, and often later conclude that we did not "worry" enough. "What shall I preach?" is a legitimate and constant question.

The potency of the gospel demands that we must preach more than the opinions of men. Argumentation on nonessentials and philosophical debate simply do not reflect the sunlight of the gospel. The comment on English preaching just before the Wesleyan revival was "Moonlight ripens no harvests."[1]

Revolution was about to erupt in the American colonies. The British Parliament had to find drastic new measures to deal with the situation or lose the New World. In that crisis hour, a lethargic King George III chose to address the legislators with his views concerning how cattle could be kept healthy.[2] It is not that the health of cattle is unimportant; but when a world is about to be lost, it is simply not a matter of primary concern. Considering the needs of my congregation, I must preach more than trivia . . . even good trivia. There is an urgency about every preaching situation that demands we deal with matters of primary concern.

The "fixed point"[3] where all our preaching starts is the fact that God has acted to reveal himself and redeem us from our sinful condition. His mighty activity in history is the presupposition of meaningful preaching.

But preaching must be more than a recounting of history—even salvation history. Preaching must be an extension of the redemptive activity of God. The power of preaching is found in the fact that at a given time God acts—present tense—through the ministry of a specific man who speaks to his fellowmen in God's name by means of the Scriptures.[4] The preacher announces the mighty activity of God in history—that the living God is present and acts redemptively in every situation.

One must then ask, "What is this redemptive activity of God, the rehearsal of which brings to pass that very activity?" Isn't God at work in all things, so that to preach His activity is to preach almost anything? Yes and no. Yes, He is active in all things. No, that does not mean that any subject is equally usable for preaching.

What then is the foundation of all Christian preaching? Our answer—God's great redemptive, creative activity is the creation, the new creation (the Christ event), and the re-creation (the second coming of the Lord Jesus). These are the major events. So if my preaching is to be a true expression of the redemptive activity of God, it must acknowledge all three dimensions. The "God who acts" is the God "who was," and "is," and "is to come."

While the chronological order of these phases of God's redemptive work is as listed above, the order of primacy is different. Priority in preaching is clearly held by the new creation—Jesus Christ, His incarnation, crucifixion, and resurrection, as well as Pentecost, which He promised and made possible. Without the Christ event the other activities of God would have no meaning. But through Him the others are illuminated with significance and hope. All, including the mysteries of the creation and the Second Coming, find their unity in Him.

1. Preaching the Christ Event—the New Creation

The request of the Greeks, "Sir, we would see Jesus," is the central request of history. To know the redemptive activity of God, I must see Jesus. Paul saw Christ on the road to Damascus and later testified, "If anyone is in Christ, he is a new creation" (2 Cor. 5:17, RSV). So we use the phrase "new creation" to refer to the total redemptive work of God revealed in the New Testament; God broke new ground there on the behalf of despairing mankind.

In our preaching it should be borne in mind that these phases of the Christ event are not separate works. Thus, while it is necessary to consider them one at a time, the Incarnation cannot have meaning without the Crucifixion, the Crucifixion cannot have meaning without the Resurrection, even as the Resurrection is incomplete without Pentecost.

It must also be remembered that it is the eternal God who is acting, even though He is acting in time. So our redemption did not really begin at Calvary, nor even at Bethlehem, but in truth, "The Lamb is slain from the foundation of the world" (Rev. 13:8).

a. The Incarnation is the act of God by which He reasserts His redemptive identification with His creation.

When God created the universe and pronounced it "good," He asserted the original moral quality of the creation. But sin defiled not only our first parents but the whole earthly setting. All might anticipate rejection and damnation from God.

It is just at this point that the incredible news of God's redemptive act in the incarnation of His Son breaks as such "good news." It is the unique fact of history. God is at work through Jesus Christ right here in the arena of human history. "The Word was made flesh and dwelt among us and we beheld his glory" (John 1:14).

It is historically true. Jesus was "born of the Virgin Mary" (the Apostles' Creed); He walked the stony hills of Galilee. A humble time and place actually knew him. "We have seen with our eyes . . . we have looked upon, and our hands have handled" (1 John 1:1) is the report of a man named John.

He has come all the way to where we are—all the way. He has taken on the form of a man. He became sin. It is incredible.

With His arrival to our hopeless place, we find hope. "The blind receive their sight, and the lame walk, the lepers are cleansed, and the deaf hear, the dead are raised up, and the poor have the gospel preached to them" (Matt. 11:5).[5] Despair is shattered; I need never be lonely, for He has come to me.

This potent Incarnation message must be preached today. It will save our preaching from becoming irrelevant and other-worldly. It declares with strong accents that God is concerned about what is happening in His world. He is concerned about pain and sickness and social injustice. Jesus will say again as He said to His first-century audience, "The time has come; the kingdom of God is upon you" (Mark 1:15, NEB). Immanuel—God with us—is still His fresh good news.

b. The Crucifixion is His demonstration of the sinfulness of men, the love of Jesus, and the will of the Father.

Paul wrote to the Galatians, "But God forbid that I should glory, save in the cross of our Lord Jesus Christ, by whom the world is crucified unto me, and I unto the world" (6:14). The Cross must always be at the center of our preaching. That is not to say that we can easily love the Cross. There is a sense in which we must despise the Cross, for it demonstrates the powers of hell. Yet only the crucified Christ can liberate from the fear of death.[6]

The three important perspectives of the Cross are listed by James Stewart in his classic book *A Faith to Proclaim.* First, the Cross reminds us that the sinister forces of hell were at work at Calvary. The obvious schemes of sinful men were actually the historic, evil elements of pride, self-love, and fear which have always been at work. The powers of darkness were there. The Cross is a cosmic battleground; it was the invisible, spiritual, demonic "rulers of the present age" that "crucified the Lord of glory" (1 Cor. 2:8).

But the Cross is also a demonstration of the love of Christ. "For when we were without strength, in due time Christ died for the ungodly. . . . But God commendeth his love toward us, in that, while we were yet sinners, Christ died for us" (Rom. 5:6, 8). These are the words of Paul. But hear the words of Jesus: "No man taketh my life from me, but I lay it down of myself" (John 10:18). He was not a helpless victim. Again He states, "Thinkest thou that I cannot pray to my Father, and he shall presently give me more than twelve legions of angels?" (Matt. 26:53). Christ suffering on the Cross was a willing expression of identifying love.

It was precisely in this fact that the forces of evil were defeated. P. T. Forsyth states it this way, "The holiness of

Christ was the one thing damnatory to the Satanic power. And it was His death which consummated that holiness. It was His death, therefore, that was Satan's final doom."[7]

Paul states in Col. 2:15, "He disarmed the principalities and powers and made a public example of them, triumphing over them at the cross." Calvin comments on that verse, "There is no tribunal so magnificent, no throne so stately, no show of triumph so distinguished, no chariot so elevated, as is the gibbet on which Christ has subdued death and the devil, and trodden them under his feet."

Not only is the Cross the demonstration of the sinfulness of men and the love of Christ, but is also a demonstration of the purpose and will of the Father. It is marvelous how the disciples soon came to see the eternal purpose at work in the Cross. Peter preached on the day of Pentecost, "By the determinate counsel and foreknowledge of God" (Acts 2:23). Paul states simply, "God was in Christ, reconciling the world unto himself" (2 Cor. 5:19). Behind and through all troublesome detail of the Cross, the love of the Son and the purpose of the Father are at work.

These three aspects of the Cross must find their way into our preaching. Not only because faithfulness to the Scriptures demands it, but because faithfulness to our people requires it. We must recognize the Cross as an expression of the forces of evil, for, while the decisive battle has been won, the conflict still rages. The people to whom we preach are subject to the attacks of the devil designed through evil people as well as by direct temptation. In such a time they must hear that Jesus Christ is their Advocate and makes full identification with their distress. Even in the midst of the murderous multitude, God is working out His purpose both faithfully and redemptively.

The message from the torn veil must be repeated by us. That elegant symbol of *deus absconditus*, which held passing generations of Jewish worshipers in awe, was rent from top to bottom. All three Gospel writers recorded it. The God of mystery, who was always hidden behind the veil, and His forlorn and unfulfilled worshipers are now brought together. God is doing a new thing.

The despairing people in our congregation desperately need to hear of the crucifixion of our Saviour and the message of sin, love, and purpose which emanates from the Cross.

c. Our Resurrection preaching is the declaration of Christ's victory.

Each of these aspects of the new creation are important, but without the Resurrection the whole Christian message falls to pieces. Paul was right. Without the empty tomb, our faith, our hope, our preaching are all vain (1 Cor. 15:14). Advent, Christmas, Epiphany, Good Friday are helpless to redeem. But with Easter they become the new creation act of God.

The early preaching of the New Testament Church was founded upon that faith (1 Cor. 15:38). If thou shalt confess with thy mouth the Lord Jesus, and shalt believe in thine heart that God hath raised him from the dead, thou shalt be saved" (Rom. 10:9). Christ is "declared to be the Son of God with power, according to the spirit of holiness, by the resurrection from the dead" (Rom. 1:4).

The twentieth-century, Western mind is desperately in need of the message of the Resurrection. The congregation is filled with many who question the triumph of good over evil, or light over darkness. There seems to be so much evidence to the contrary. In the midst of such foreboding conditions, they need to hear preaching like the proclamation of the first century which declared the victory of Jesus Christ over death, hell, and the grave. The Scriptures recall ancient confessions, "Now Christ is risen from the dead, and become the firstfruits of them that slept. . . . For as in Adam all die, even so in Christ shall all be made alive. . . . Thanks be to God, which giveth us the victory through our Lord Jesus Christ" (1 Cor. 15:20, 22, 57).

But as we preach these truths, the power of God makes them live again. Modern hearts will conclude, "I live because He lives." Only the power of the resurrected Jesus, giving evidence of His vitality within the preaching and worship of the congregation, will meet current needs. The crisis hour that we face demands that every preaching effort announce again the redemptive work of God.

d. The preaching of the new creation is not complete without the message of Pentecost.

The writer of Hebrews makes it clear that the ultimate purpose of Christ's redemptive work was the sanctification of the believer. "Wherefore Jesus also, that he might sancitfy the people with his own blood, suffered without the gate" (Heb. 13:12). Our preaching of the Christ event cannot be complete unless it clearly sounds the New Testament message of the coming and indwelling of the blessed Holy Spirit. Jesus said, "Nevertheless I tell you the truth; it is expedient for you that I go away: for if I go not away, the Comforter will not come unto you; but if I depart, I will send him unto you. And when he is come, he will reprove the world of sin, and of righteousness, and of judgment" (John 16:7–8). Here Christ insisted that His full work was to be continued by the Third Person of the Trinity.

It is imperative, then, that our preaching reflect the full power of the new creation. The Incarnation with its assertion of redemptive activity in the arena of human history; the Crucifixion with its message of the sinfulness of man, the love of Christ, and the purpose of the Father; the glorious Resurrection with its declaration of God's victory for us over every enemy—all must shout from our pulpits every time we address our needy people. Every message must reflect these truths, but no less the message of Pentecost.

There must be this essential coherence in the various dimensions of our Christ-event preaching. If one aspect of His redemptive work is neglected, the other aspects somehow become less powerful. Our waiting congregation must hear not only of the incarnation, crucifixion, and resurrection of our Lord; they must also hear that He has sent the Holy Spirit and that the Holy Spirit has arrived to indwell the waiting heart of the believer, sanctifying and bringing under His lordship all the wondering ambitions of the soul.

If "Jesus' light" does not shine on the message, it is a dark message.

2. Preaching the Character of God—the First Creation

Preach about the creation? Perhaps this does not appear to be a dominant theme of the modern pulpit. But remember that our basic task as preachers is to declare the mighty acts of God. Then consider how basic the creative work of God is to the Scriptures. The Genesis account of creation sets the pattern for all the Old Testament. The God who creates, determining all things and determined by none (*ex nihilo*),[9] drawing order out of the void, is also the God who with mighty power calls out a people who are no people. He delivers them from the slavery of the past and promises to walk with them into the future. By the time you finish preaching the creation stories of Genesis, a great deal has already been said about the essential character of God and how He acts.

Any preacher who misses the basic connection between the new creation and the first creation has overlooked a rich and basic insight. When John begins his story about the redemptive life of Jesus, he feels compelled by the Holy Spirit to retell the first creation story. He understands that the redemptive power that brought the worlds into existence is precisely the power that is at work in Jesus of Nazareth.[10]

> In the beginning was the Word, and the Word was with God, and the Word was God. The same was in the beginning with God. All things were made by him; and without him was not anything made that was made. In him was life; and the life was the light of men. . . . That was the true Light, which lighteth every man that cometh into the world. He was in the world, and the world was made by him, and the world knew [received] him not. . . . But as many as received him, to them gave he power to become the sons of God (*John 1:1–4, 9–12*).

The last book of the Scriptures repeats the same theme:

> I am Alpha and Omega, the first and the last. . . . Holy, holy, holy, Lord God Almighty, which was, and is, and is to come. . . . Thou art worthy, O Lord, to receive glory and honour and power: for thou hast created all things, and for thy pleasure they are and were created (*Rev. 1:11; 4:8, 11*).

This awareness of the eternal, creative, and redemptive purposes of God is basic to preaching with authority. Contemporary man has been educated, by and large, in an atmosphere which refuses to make any statements concerning eternal purpose. The absence of such a faith has resulted in widespread despair. Our gathered congregations need to hear of the mighty activity of God. The eternal God is at work and has been since, yes, even before the creation. He is the same God who acted in Christ Jesus.

3. Preaching the Second Coming—the Creation Yet to Be

The passage from Revelation quoted above stated, "I am Alpha and Omega, the first and the last.... Lord God Almighty, which was, and is, and is to come." It is clear from the biblical perspective that the God who acted in creation and who acted in the "new creation" has not now left us to our own destinies. The redemptive purposes which have been at work from the beginning are not exhausted now. He not only continues to manifest the creative powers invested in the "first creation" and the "new creation," but the time will come in human history when He will again do a truly new thing; He will come again—"the creation yet to be."

The New Testament preachers looked forward to this event because they anticipated it as redemptive just as the first creation and the new creation had been. It was not, therefore, set aside for conversations about last things: Rather, it was an anticipation of the continued activity of their redemptive God shining new light on all living. In the light of the Second Coming they were admonished to be watchful and sober (Mark 13:33; Rev. 16:15; 1 Thes. 5:6), faithful (Luke 12:42–44; 19:12–26; Mark 8:38), to live lives of moderation not too attached to the world (Matt. 16:26–27; Phil. 1:9–10; 4:5; Col. 3:2–5), to be patient (Heb. 10:36–37; Jas. 5:7–8), and live lives of holiness (1 Thess. 3:12–13; 5:28; 1 John 2:28; 2 Pet. 3:11–13; Titus 2:11–13). All of these references and many more illustrate that the Second Coming faith was not a fascination about "when," "how," and "under what circumstance." Faith in the Jesus who "was" and "is" was inseparable from hope

101

for the Jesus who "is to come." A doctrine of Christ is incomplete without the Second Coming.

Their lives were no naive detachment from the world—quite the contrary. They suffered great physical hardships. But they steadfastly declared that the God whom they served is the God who had acted in the arena of human affairs, creating the world with the power of His might. They believed that the birth of every child and the blooming of every plant was an evidence of that creative God.

They further believed that the Eternal Word, through whom the first creation was realized, became flesh, was crucified, dead, and buried, but the third day rose again. In this redemptive act He broke new ground. Every redeemed person then is a new creation.

But this is not the end for the New Testament preachers. This same Jesus will come again . . . right here in the center of human history where His other creative acts have occurred. When He comes, He will "make all things new" (Rev. 21:5). There is much that we of the old order cannot know about the new order. But we clearly declare that the God who created the existing order, who then, in the fullness of time, brought into reality the new creation in Christ Jesus, will someday again act creatively and redemptively. His is the power of consummation.

All of His creative activity reflects the constancy of His character. All is redemptive. All is "truly new." All relates to the human life arena in which we find ourselves. It is impossible to think of the God who "was" and "is" without thinking of the God who "is to come."

A good surveyor can direct his course through seemingly unconquerable mountain terrain if he can fix his sextant on three dependable distant landmarks. The biblical preacher has three fixed points for his preaching—the first creation, the Christ event, and the Second Advent.

True, our world is confused because it has lost its dependable distant landmarks. But our preaching can bring the people back to these foundation facts of the Christian faith. The basis of preaching can be nothing less than the mighty redemptive activity of God . . . the new creation . . . the first creation . . . and the creation yet to come. Every message that we preach must accurately reflect those longitudinal and latitudinal lines. Even when our subject does not relate primarily to these, the relationship must be clear and definite.

What shall I preach? is a basic, haunting, frequent question. The answer: "Preach the mighty acts of God . . . new creation, first creation, and the creation yet to come."

● **Leslie Evans**

7

Preaching Great Bible Doctrines

In the preface to his volume of sermons on *Christian Doctrine*, Dr. Dale tells an interesting story about himself. Three or four years after he had settled in Carr's Lane, he was in the streets of Birmingham when he met another Congregational minister. His friend was a Welshman with all the Welshman's love for imagination and poetry, and, perhaps, a Welshman's dread of hard logic and dry reason. Being a much older man than Dale, the Welshman spoke freely to him about his preaching. "I hear that you are preaching doctrinal sermons to the congregation at Carr's Lane. They will not stand it." To which Dale promptly replied: "They will have to stand it."

Throughout Dale's long and noble ministry, they not only stood it but welcomed it and rejoiced in it. Was ever a pulpit devoted to mightier themes than when Dale filled it? Every chapter of his book on the atonement went through his pulpit, and it was so of his great work on Ephesians.

John A. Broadus says:

> Doctrine, i.e. teaching, is the preacher's chief business. Truth is the life-blood of piety, without which we cannot maintain its vitality or support its activity. And to teach men truth, or to quicken what they already know into freshness and power, is the preacher's greatest means of doing good.[1]

Definition of Doctrinal Preaching

The very word *doctrinal* is somewhat forbidding, and it would be helpful to make it clear that it simply means a "teaching" sermon. There is a sense in which all true biblical preaching is doctrinal preaching, for all biblical truth relates in some way to the great doctrines of our faith.

But "doctrinal preaching aims at instructing the people methodically in the truths of the Gospel."[2] It will take up the great themes of the Scriptures: Sin, Forgiveness, Atonement, Regeneration, Providence, Judgment, and so on. As J. W. Alexander puts it neatly in *Thoughts on Preaching*: "Christian doctrines are but the truths of Christianity."[3]

Doctrinal preaching consists of the great saving objective truths of the gospel, which are the mighty acts of God wrought once for all in history, and of the great subjective work of the Holy Spirit within us, which is the fulfillment of God's mighty acts in the experience of the believer. Its whole theme is salvation—a saving God and a saved people.

There are two words given for "doctrine" or "teaching" in the New Testament; together they occur more than 50 times. Christ was himself addressed as Teacher," and in His ministry He was par excellence the Teacher, "a teacher from God." Of the Early Church after Pentecost we read: "They continued steadfastly in the apostles' doctrine and fellowship, and in breaking of bread, and in prayers" (Acts 2:42). The order of priority is significant. Preaching formed the Early Church, but teaching bound it. Christian doctrine has been described as "the fundamental truths of revelation arranged in systematic form." It is the setting out of right beliefs about God. Knowledge by itself gets no man to God, but it plays a powerful part in our life of faith.

The Need for Doctrinal Preaching

1. The need for doctrinal preaching springs from *the essential nature of the Christian ministry*. In the Great Commission, Jesus said to His disciples; "Go ye therefore, and teach all nations ... teaching them to asverve all things whatsoever I have commanded you" (Matt. 28:19–20). When Paul writes on the duties and responsibilities of the Christian ministry, he says: "All scripture is given by inspiration by God, and is profitable for doctrine, for reproof, for correction, for instruction in righteousness" (2 Tim. 3:16). Commenting on the words "apt to teach" (1 Tim. 3:2), William Barclay says:

> It is one of the disasters of modern times that the teaching ministry of the church has not been exercised as it should. There is any amount of topical preaching; there is any amount of exhortation; but there is little use in exhorting a man to be a Christian if he does not know what being a Christian means. Instruction is a primary duty of the Christian preacher."[4]

Such is the ignorance of the Bible in these days that when a schoolteacher came to the end of her scripture lesson on the "trial" of Jesus, her class urged her to continue so that they would know whether He was released or not. It is a common occurrence for ordinary people not to know what Whitsun celebrates. It is fast becoming perilous to

106

assume that our people already know the basic facts of our faith. Writing of his preconversion experience, David Sheppard, recently appointed bishop of Liverpool, says: "Preachers had often been assuming far too much knowledge, and Christian experience, and had therefore left me lost and unmoved."[5]

2. Another reason for the need to preach the great doctrines of the Bible is *the need to combat error.* Horton Davies, in his book *Christian Deviations: The Challenge of the Sects,* takes up the description of the sects as being "the unpaid bills of the churches," and points to lack of clear teaching as being part of that "unpaid bill." Certainly, the best way to repudiate the false is to assert the true. Once a man gets hold of the positive truth, false and misleading ideas become innocuous.

It is a sad but true fact that the Christian Church has often failed to pronounce the true beliefs clearly and compellingly. A Jehovah's Witness said at a mass rally, when asked why she had become a member, "I tried seven different churches and none of them could answer my questions. When I met the Witnesses, they could give me an answer. They showed me that the Bible has an answer for everything." It has indeed an answer, but the other churches failed to expound its teaching faithfully.

When saying good-bye to the elders of the Ephesian church at Miletus, Paul said, "I have not shunned to declare unto you all the counsel of God. Take heed therefore ... For I know this that after my departing shall grievous wolves enter in among you, not sparing the flock" (Acts 20:27–29). Those wolves are still at work, and the faith is best defended by the positive proclamation of the great truths of the Bible.

In that marvelously vital and challenging book, *A Faith to Proclaim,* James Stewart writes: "The fact remains that the greatest drag on Christianity today, the most serious menace to the Church's mission, is not the secularism without, it is the reduced Christianity within: the religious generalities and innocuous platitudes of a pallid, anaemic Christianity."[6]

If we think that our people know the faith, it might be a humbling experience, as Sangster suggests, to ask them to explain "How does God forgive us?" or "Why do you believe in the personality of the Holy Spirit?" or "How does the Cross save us?"[7]

We cannot edify the church or combat error adequately without sound teaching. There are those who see little need for doctrinal preaching, referring to such preaching as being "mere bones." But what sort of body would there be which was flesh and blood without bones?

3. A further need for doctrinal preaching lies in the fact that *a strong teaching ministry will stimulate expectation, and expectation makes possible experience.* To teach biblical doctrine is to set forth what God is and does, and opens the door to a wider and deeper life with Him.

Henry Sloan Coffin stresses this important element in doctrinal preaching by pointing out that Paul found a group of earnest men at Ephesus who were followers of John the Baptist, but who knew nothing of the possession of the Spirit. Their meagre theology limited their experience. Paul's teaching on Jesus and the Spirit enabled them to enter into a new experience.[8] Thus doctrine can stimulate expectation, awaken desire, and greatly enrich faith and experience. The great biblical doctrines are to be looked at, but we are to look through them in order to see more clearly the nature of God, the work of Christ, and life in the Spirit. So many people today have a moral squint or are spiritually shortsighted simply because their vision is not rectified by sound doctrine.

4. Doctrinal preaching is necessary for *a true evangelical ministry*. In a pamphlet published by the Methodist Local Preachers Department, entitled *Doctrinal Preaching*, the point is made that doctrinal preaching is evangelical preaching.

Two factors contributed supremely to the Evangelical Revival of the 18th century—John Wesley's preaching and Charles Wesley's hymns. Both these were firmly based on Christian doctrine. Far from being dull, abstract or academic, whether mediated through sermons or hymns, Christian doctrine is the very foundation and source of all true evangelism.[9]

Andrew Blackwood supports this view, stating that "in the past every evangelistic movement blessed of God has come largely through preaching doctrine." When we think of the vocabulary of evangelism—sin, repent, save, faith, conversion—all of these words and many more have to be filled with content and meaning.

It is significant that Samuel Chadwick, one-time principal of Cliff College, preached steadily through Pope's *Compendium of Theology* and always had large crowds to hear him. He not only filled churches, he led thousands into a real experience of Christ. In his own words, "The course on 'The Apostles' Creed' held them for ten successive Sunday nights, and I am still of the opinion that the preaching most appreciated by the crowd is sound theology, vitalised by experience."[10]

Doctrinal preaching will save us from that modern form of an old heresy which claims that it doesn't matter what you believe so long as your heart is in the right place. "By grace are ye saved through faith; and that not of yourselves, it is the gift of God" (Eph. 2:8). Our preaching must offer that grace and define that faith.

The Difficulties of Doctrinal Preaching

1. Perhaps one of the major difficulties of doctrinal preaching is *the need to make sure that it is doctrinal preaching*. It must be truth set firmly in the context of a sermon. This means that all the principles and vital elements that make preaching what it is must be applied to doctrinal preaching. Doctrinal preaching is not a theological lecture. The sermon must be a sermon.

2. *The difficulty of communicating doctrine*. There are those who object to doctrinal preaching on the ground that it tends to be dry. But this is true of any kind of preaching. As Sangster says, "Some men could make any subject dry. Their capacity for dehydration is unlimited."[11]

Archbishop Magee used to say, "There are sermons you cannot listen to, there are sermons you can listen to, and there are sermons you cannot help listening to." We need not be numbered among those who take pride in the "dignity of dullness."

Preachers sometimes hesitate to deal with great Bible doctrines because they are afraid that their doctrines may not be logically flawless. Passionate utterance is no substitute for sound doctrine; a heart strangely warmed is no excuse for a head strangely empty. But we must remember that we do not need to grasp *all* the implications of our faith before we preach it; for who, then, would preach? We do not need to be professors of theology before we confront the people with saving faith—but we must learn to communicate the truths we have grasped, we must learn to translate our theological terms into language which can be readily understood.

The purpose of true preaching is not simply to announce truth, but to communicate truth, and a man is not preaching when this is not so. Ilion Jones tells the following story:

> One minister described the following as the most disconcerting experience of his ministry. As he began his sermon an elderly woman, seated near the front, opened a little box, took out an elaborate hearing device, arranged its parts, screwed them together, and adjusted the receiver to her ear. After listening for a few minutes she removed the receiver, took the device apart, repacked it in the box, and sat quietly in the pew for the remainder of the sermon. Many people, who have no hearing devices, have ways of shutting out the sermon as effectively as that woman. When that happens, the Gospel may have been proclaimed, but it has not been communicated.[12]

There is nothing more exasperating for the man in the pew than to be addressed in words and ideas he does not understand. It all goes over his head. As Spurgeon put it, "The Lord said, 'Feed my sheep,' not 'Feed my giraffes.' " An English preacher began his sermon to a congregation in India with the sentence "Now faith is both abstract and concrete." The interpreter translated: "So far the minister hasn't said anything, but when he does, I'll let you know." So often, as far as our people are concerned, we are not saying anything. Those who preach doctrine must clarify thought and simplify language, so that all can hear—in their own tongue—the wonderful works of God.

3. *The difficulty of relevance and application.* As in all preaching, doctrinal preaching must be related to the present situation. "Preaching is not the self-expression of the preacher. Preaching implies a congregation. And the necessity lies in the nature of preaching. What makes preaching possible therefore is the existence of men in

need and the existence of a remedy to meet that need. Preaching is the link between these two."[13]

The difficulty of doctrinal preaching is to make sure that we keep that vital link. It is possible to preach doctrine in such a way that it appears that it has no connection with life at all, and a sermon that has nothing to do with life is certain to be uninteresting.

A. W. Tozer puts it this way:

There is scarcely anything so dull and meaningless as Bible doctrine taught for its own sake. Truth divorced from life is not truth in the Biblical sense, but something else and something less. . . . No man is better for knowing that God in the beginning created the heaven and the earth. The devil knows that, and so did Ahab and Judas Iscariot. No man is better for knowing God so loved the world of men that He gave His only begotten Son for their redemption. In hell there are millions who know that. Theological truth is useless until it is obeyed. The purpose behind all doctrine is to secure moral action.[14]

The Apostles' Creed presents the basic, fundamental beliefs of the Christian faith, rooted in the Bible and relevant to life. A sermon on the first article of the Creed—"I believe in God the Father Almighty, maker of heaven and earth"—might have the first verse of the Bible as its text, "In the beginning God created the heaven and the earth." The Christian doctrine of creation is less concerned with the age of the rocks and the problem of evolution than with the present fact that if God is the Creator, we are dependent on Him, and that we are stewards and not owners of all that God has made. This is a belief which has far-reaching consequences in our living; it affects life at many points, and it cannot be dry or dull unless we make it so.

Doctrinal preaching makes the preacher and the congregation think; but it must do more than that, or it has

112

failed of its true purpose. We should do well to ask, before we begin to prepare a doctrinal sermon; "What difference does it really make to me if I believe this?" There ought to be a clear answer to that question, for if we don't know, it is certain our hearers will not when we have finished. Each of the great objectivities of the faith—"what God hath wrought" once for all in history—has its implication in our Christian experience—what God wills to work in us and through us. It is for this reason that the New Testament follows up each proclamation of doctrine with a very practical "therefore" (e.g., Rom. 12:1). As John Wesley said, "God loves you, therefore love and obey Him: Christ died for you, therefore die to sin: Christ is risen, therefore rise in the image of God: Christ liveth for evermore, therefore live to God till you live with Him in glory."

James Stalker points out that Paul unites doctrine with duty in all his letters, that he always takes the step from creed to conduct.

> In Paul's mind all the great doctrines of the Gospel were living fountains of motives for well doing: and even the smallest and commonest duties of everyday life were magnified and made sacred by being connected with the facts of salvation. Take a simple instance. There is no plainer duty in everyday life than telling the truth. Well, how does Paul treat it? "Lie not one to another," he says, "seeing ye have put off the old man with his deeds." Thus, truthfulness flows out of regeneration.[15]

We must not present doctrine as mere abstract truth with a take-it-or-leave-it attitude, or the expectation that our hearers will make the application themselves. It is our responsibility to make the vital connection with life, for it is at that point the message comes alive. As Spurgeon says, "The sermon begins where the application begins." The primary purpose of preaching must be kept very firmly in mind—that through it God may work a transformation in human lives. "A preacher preaching a sermon without application would be like a physician giving to his patient a lecture on general health, and forgetting to write him a prescription."

When George Fox stirred people violently by his preaching in the seventeenth century, he often used a phrase in his journal: "I spoke to their condition." Doctrinal preaching certainly speaks to the condition of our age, and of any age. When a preacher takes up the great Bible doctrines, he is preaching, not only to the times, but to the eternities.

Examples of Doctrinal Preaching

It is vitally important that when we preach great Bible doctrines, we establish them on a solid foundation. This means that we are careful in our selection of the Bible passage which is to carry the weight of the doctrine preached. It is possible to use God's Word in a trivial fashion.

Ilion T. Jones tells of a minister who spoke of Jacob crossing his arms over two of Joseph's children when he blessed them (Gen. 48:13–14) and drawing from the incident the theme: "There is not blessing but under the Cross." Another preacher took Esau's question directed to Isaac: "Hast thou but one blessing, my father?" and proceeded to try to build a doctrinal sermon on sanctification as a distinct, second work of grace. In both cases it is not the doctrine but the biblical basis that we question. Dr. Dale said that when he watched such preachers developing doctrines and interesting speculations from texts by this process, he was always reminded of the tricks of a conjurer—and that is not our calling.

Another area of doubt is reached when we approach narrative portions of the Bible. Are we drawing the correct conclusion from the story? Is an incident recorded as a warning or as an example? If it is an example, is it normal or exceptional? It is a principle of biblical interpretation that biblical events may illustrate biblical doctrine, but they do not, in themselves, constitute biblical doctrine. It is wise to interpret biblical events in the light of the established doctrine of the Scriptures.

As an example of this principle let us take the doctrine of the Holy Spirit. It is possible to try to build a doctrine from the events of Acts, but are these events normal in Christian experience or exceptional? (We do not expect to reproduce today all the physical phenomena of the Day of Pentecost.) For purposes of doctrinal preaching it is far safer to go to the teaching passages of the New Testament, such as John 14; 15; 16; Romans 8; 1 Corinthians 12; and many more.

In a volume of sermons entitled *The Strong Name*, James S. Stewart reveals the powers of doctrinal preaching. Great themes are dealt with—Reconciliation, The Nature of Jesus, The Lord's Supper, The Trinity, Immortality, Suffering. This is doctrinal preaching at its best—vitally relevant, Bible-based, wonderfully illustrated, and always gripping.

One of the sermons is entitled "The Gospel of the Ascension," in which Stewart deals with the practical meaning of the event. He takes three texts: Luke 24:51–53; John 16:7; Eph. 4:8. His development of the theme is as follows:

Introduction. The sadness and sorrow of parting for those who love each other. The astonishing words of Luke—"Jesus was parted from them . . . and they returned to Jerusalem with great joy." Jesus had said, "It is expedient for you that I go away," and now they knew it was expedient.

115

(1) *For the spiritualizing of religion.* If He had stayed, they would have remained dependent on His visible presence. "If I go not away the Spirit will not come."

(2) *For the universalizing of the gospel.* While Christ was with His disciples, He could not belong to all the world.

(3) *For the energizing of evangelism.* Take the magnificent metaphor of Paul to the Church: "Ye are the body of Christ." Without the Ascension that conception would never have arisen.

(4) *For the fortifying of faith.* "He led captivity captive"—He was triumphant—the disciples knew He had conquered.[16]

Every point has relevance and application combined with teaching on the meaning of the Ascension.

Another example of doctrinal preaching is to be found in a sermon by Ian Macpherson with the title "Jesus Is the Atonement." The text is Rom. 5:11, "Jesus Christ, by whom we have now received the atonement [reconciliation]."

In the introduction, Macpherson tells of the Welsh theologian Dr. Edwards, of Bala, who, while writing his book on the atonement, suddenly received a beam of revelation. It set his soul on fire; and running into the street, he shouted, "Jesus *is* the Atonement." Then going back to his study, he wrote: "This is the Atonement—not the sufferings and not the death. It is not that He made the Atonement or paid the Atonement. The Bible goes beyond that. He *is* the Atonement."

(1) *Christ unites God and man in His person*—we are brought face-to-face with the uniqueness of Jesus.

116

(2) *Christ unites God and man in His passion*—Love's redeeming work was accomplished at the Cross.

(3) *Christ unites God and man by His presence*—He comes to live in our hearts—"I live, yet not I, Christ liveth in me."[17]

This message on reconciliation has a strong evangelical appeal, supported by strong biblical truth.

Sometimes the doctrinal sermon can be a straightforward exposition of a verse or section of scripture which is itself a statement of faith. A sermon on the "Providence of God," for example, could be based on Paul's discovery that his imprisonment was not the unmitigated disaster his Philippian friends tended to think it was. Paul pointed out that his bonds were made manifest in the palace, his prison wardens were brought within the sound of the gospel, and his Christian brothers were made confident in the faith. From many viewpoints, Paul could say that what had happened to him had "fallen out rather unto the furtherance of the gospel" (Phil. 1:12). From the point of view of later history we have even greater cause to thank God for Paul's imprisonment, since it was through his enforced withdrawal from pioneer missionary work that his priceless letters were written to guide and encourage the believers of his day. A similar sermon with the same theme could be preached from the story of Joseph.

W. E. Sangster's summation at this point is pertinent:

The very craft of preaching is to take the technological facts and make them shine with immense significance and become the glowing truths by which men live. Here, then, is the preacher's task: to preach about God, to show man his own real nature, to expose sin, to announce the way of salvation . . . to hold up in a hundred ways the wonder of atonement,

117

to tell of the work of the Holy Spirit, and to proclaim all the refinements of grace. Teaching—preaching deals with centralities. And no sustained ministry is worthy which fails to do that.[18]

The preacher's ultimate aim is not to produce great sermons, but to make great Christians. "Every sermon should be an agony of soul, a passion to beget Christ in the souls of men." Preaching marginal things or toying with trifles will never accomplish this supreme purpose. We are called to proclaim "mercy's whole design," to make known the great truths of God's Word, and any failure at this point is failure at every point of our preaching ministry.

● Darrell E. Luther

8

Making Life-Situation Preaching Biblical

Many parishioners come each Sunday with a hope their pastor will answer one crucial question. It is substantially the same question an ancient king secretly put to a prophet in a time of difficulty: "Is there any word from the Lord?" (Jer. 37:17). It is the universal quest for a solution to life's perplexing riddle. Is there any fresh word from God to help resolve the tensions, relieve the pressures, provide an antidote for worry, and eradicate the sense of guilt which plagues every man in this age of anxiety and fear? In short, is there a word that God cares about me?

The preacher stands between the grace of God and man's needs. His task is to bring the two together, not by more preaching, but by better preaching. The preaching we need will be fuller and more practical; it will answer the real questions of human existence.

Ideally, like electrodes in an arc light, the sermon

119

should bring the affirmations of the Bible and life issues together. Faris Whitesell emphasizes this need: "The preacher should be able to feel the pulse and sense the mood of the age in which he lives. To do this, he must be in touch with the currents of life and thought. Such understanding will help him slant his preaching to today's world rather than to yesterday's."[1]

Paul Scherer brings the eternal demand of the Bible and contemporary need of man together when he says the Bible is *his* Book, "not simply because it is the story of what happened once, but also because in it and through it and by way of it everything is happening now."[2]

Karl Barth, the Swiss theologian, insists that God makes himself known in three ways: supremely in Christ, largely through the Bible, and through the present-day preacher.[3] If he is accurate, then the preacher himself deeply influences his preaching.

Frame of Reference

The pastor's preaching ministry is greatly determined by the geography of his mind and the perimeter of his experience. This is known as a frame of reference. This consists of a system of values which to some extent control actions and determine his expression of attitudes or beliefs. Thus, within a pastor's frame of reference, certain considerations are accepted and others refused—often with no thought of why.

1. *Self-esteem*

Implicitly within the preacher's frame of reference is his personal valuation of his own worth—his self-esteem. No value judgment is more important to the preacher and nothing more motivating than his own estimate of himself.

This estimate is usually experienced not in the form of a conscious, verbalized judgment, but reflects a self-appraisal either beneficial or harmful that he has made of himself. Self-esteem has two interrelated aspects—self-confidence and self-respect.

Through the redemption offered by Jesus Christ, one is competent to live and worthy of living—even the preacher. This basic self-confidence is not a judgment passed on how many years he attended school or the number of degrees he holds. Neither is it based on skills one may have learned. Rather the preacher's self-esteem is in the context of his understanding of a personal God as revealed through Jesus Christ. It is the confidence he enjoys as a result of his belief that he is created in the image of God, has been redeemed by the love of God, and through this relationship God is interested, involved, and is responding to his personal needs. Self-esteem provides the confidence needed for the preacher to relate openly to his people.

2. Honesty

To be accepted, we tend to play the roles imposed upon us by people around us. It is tragic when the result is chronic self-deception. We become, then, an artificial person. Personal dishonesty is an insidious disease. Like cancer, it eats away until a person becomes unaware of the basic truths about himself. Are we honest in our preaching when we say we trust God, but doubt that He will help us in our crises?

Ananias and Sapphira are biblical examples of self-deception. Even though they kept the stated rules, pretense was a way of life for them. They dropped dead at First Church. Spiritual laws are such that when we are not honest with ourselves and others, physical, emotional, or spiritual death is inevitable.

121

Self-discovery is a fascinating, satisfying, and sometimes painful experience. God is not shocked by our emotional hang-ups. Even the people who comprise our congregations will understand if at times we share how God helped us through a difficult situation or brought help in time of need.

Honesty is essential to Christian growth, and self-awareness is a primary ingredient of personal effectiveness. Honesty is contagious. But how does one begin to discover himself?

a. Start with a realistic look at yourself, noting strengths and weaknesses. Don't go through life as a complete stranger to yourself.

b. Mirror yourself in the Bible. Measure your real self against its standards.

c. Look at yourself through the eyes of real friends.

The Bible proclaims, "If we walk in the light [light reveals; darkness conceals] as he is in the light, we have fellowship." Our objective is not morbid introspection but an inward look for the purposes of knowing ourselves, becoming more like Jesus, and identifying with our people in the pew.

While president of Nazarene Theological Seminary, Dr. L. T. Corlett shared a startling idea with his students. He said one could never be a great pastor until he had first suffered. He then continued, "I pray that if you have not suffered before, you will suffer in your first pastorate." After the pastor has suffered, he can begin to identify in honesty with the needs of hurting people.

Commitment to the Authority of Scripture

Three major spiritual crises have been of incalculable worth in shaping my ministry. The first was asking Christ to forgive my sins. Christ became my Saviour. The second crisis was the yielding of my independent self to the will of God. The Holy Spirit filled me and He became sanctifying Lord. The third major crisis which shaped my life was submitting my university graduate studies to the scrutiny of the Scriptures. There are illuminating insights in many fields of study, but we need biblical authority as a touchstone for all our learning. I committed my mind to the authority of the Bible as the final Solution for the needs of man.

A pastor speaks with power when he believes in the authority of the Scriptures to meet human need. This doesn't mean he is a biblicist, nor will he treat the Bible like a book of magic. Though not an idol to be worshipped, the Bible is a means of instruction. The preacher must allow the Bible to be its own authority as it speaks to human need.

The Bible is a record of the dynamic encounter of God with man in real-life situations. Belief in the authority of the Scriptures and careful Bible study allow the Word to spring to life so the preacher shares J. B. Phillips' excitement:

> I was dealing with material which was startling alive.... It was the sustained, down-to-earth faith of the New Testament writers which conveyed to me that inexpressible sense of the genuine and authentic.... It is my serious conclusion we have, in the New Testament, words that bear the hallmark of reality and ring of truth.[4]

Our work is not completed until the divine-human encounter contained in the Scriptures faces modern man in his setting and forces him to a decision. The effective, present-day preacher leads his people to be vital New Testament Christians in the twentieth century.

Awareness of Basic Human Needs

"Whoever will become a preacher must feel the needs of men until it becomes an obsession of his soul" is the way Leslie Tizard said it.[5] The preacher needs an understanding of basic human needs if he is to speak to these needs from God's Word. This obsession forces us to an elementary understanding of human behaviour.

Human beings are not merely physical organisms; neither are they mere psychological beings functioning through subconscious and conscious processes; they are all this and more—immortal souls. Forces which affect the individual's whole life are his basic needs, which include love, belonging, attention, appreciation, discipline, sex, and God. To these needs must be added the basic physical needs of water, food, and self-preservation.

Basic needs often cause frustration because of our inability to cope with stress. When thinking of stress, we usually focus our interest on three general types—frustration, conflict, and pressure. Frustration occurs when the ability to achieve a desired goal is blocked. Conflict differs from frustration in that there is more than one goal, and choice must be made between the two (or among several). Pressure involves demands that force one to intensify his efforts.

In a recent study by Dr. Thomas Holmes to the American Association for the Advancement of Science, there is evidence that too many changes, coming too close together, often produce depression or illness. From the research, Holmes devised a scale assigning point values to changes that effect human beings. When enough of these occur within one year, and add up to more than 300, trouble usually follows.[6]

Life Event	Value
Death of spouse	100
Divorce	73
Marital separation	65
Jail term	63
Death of close family member	63
Personal injury or illness	53
Marriage	50
Fired at work	47
Marital reconciliation	45
Retirement	45
Change in health of family member	44
Pregnancy	40
Sex difficulties	39
Gain of new family member	39
Change in financial state	38
Death of close friend	37
Change to different line of work	36
Change in number of arguments with spouse	35
Mortgage over $10,000	31
Foreclosure of mortgage or loan	30
Change in responsibilities of work	29
Son or daughter leaving home	29
Trouble with in-laws	29
Outstanding personal achievement	28
Wife beginning or stopping work	26
Beginning or ending school	26
Revision of personal habits	24
Trouble with boss	23
Change in work hours or conditions	20
Change in residence	20
Change in schools	20
Change in recreation	19
Change in social activities	18
Mortgage or loan less than $10,000	17
Change in sleeping habits	16
Change in number of family get-togethers	15

Many of these changes are frequently experienced by both the pastor and the members of his congregation. A simple study of this list makes preachers more aware of the needs of the people who occupy the pews.

It is obvious that inner needs affect both one's ability to preach and to receive the gospel. After a pastor finished his morning sermon, one man may say, "Good sermon; I think that was the first time I really heard the gospel." A few minutes later someone else who has been present in the same service says with equal sincerity, "Well, you've preached some good ones, but that one really missed. Be sure and preach the Bible, young man."

When these kinds of contradictory responses to the same sermon first begin to appear, one could conclude it was because people had very different intellectual conceptions of the gospel. Probably true. But the difference in responses has more to do with the different levels of need in the life of the hearer.

The famous psychologist Abraham Maslow, though not a believer, stated that a person begins life with a dominant set of overall needs which motivate his behavior and shape his thinking.[7] His theory helps us to better understand the needs of the people to whom we preach. Until these basic needs are provided for in a reliable, continuing manner, a person's life will be dominated by them. He will not be deeply interested in other things while this domination lasts. When the first cluster of needs has been dependably met, Maslow believed that a new and higher set of dominating requirements would take over the motivating center of one's life. The following diagram is a model of Maslow's hierarchy of needs.

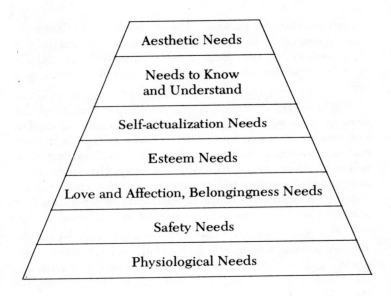

The basic set of needs which motivate people is what Maslow called *physiological needs*—the need for food, oxygen, temporal regulations, thirst satisfaction, rest, sex, and elimination. If these needs are dominant, then the person will spend much of his time trying to meet these physical needs. Furthermore, these needs will likely shape his religious concerns. He would likely be singing, "A tent or a cottage, why should I care? They're building a mansion for me over there." He believes heaven to be an eternal banquet table.

As one's physical needs are met, a new cluster of dominant needs will now occupy his attention. These Maslow referred to as *safety needs*, which include needs for physical shelter, economic security, emotional stability, and preference for the familiar. These needs also affect religious concerns so this person may understand God only as One who keeps him from harm. He would particularly enjoy a preaching emphasis of saving man from death and hell.

When safety requirements have been met, then the *need for love, affection,* and the sense of *belonging* tend to become the focus in one's life. When a person is getting enough to eat and feels safe in his world, he then begins to relate to other people in a different way. He wants to be loved, have feelings of acceptance—both giving and receiving. People with these needs relate to a sermon that states, "God loves me and accepts me just as I am."

The next cluster of needs is known as *esteem needs.* In such needs, man is in search of self-respect, status, recognition, and approval. When highly motivated with esteem needs, one's religious emphasis would probably be the feeling of a great sense of worth and being highly valued by God and other people, not because of really superior performance or possessions, but simply for himself. A preacher who talked about hellfire would miss the basic needs of such a person almost totally, whereas a speaker who emphasized that because you have worth to God you are "somebody," might hit the listener right in the heart.

After these needs have been met, Maslow then states man enters the stage of *self-actualization needs.* These needs include desire for creativity, mature relationships, deep religious expressions, and feelings of growth. A person in this stage may change his life-style. He is afraid of the unknown and has enough of his basic needs met to risk letting down his mask of unreality. As one lets down his facades, he begins to get in touch with his hopes and dreams.

Maslow's studies reveal that people who reach the stage of self-actualization are as rare as Olympic gold medal winners in the total population of athletes. He did not find a single case of a self-actualizer under 50 years of age. However, he did not take into consideration the power of Christ to change people. Some great Christians were converted and displayed a number of self-actualizing characteristics years before their fiftieth birthday. Men such as Augustine, Luther, and Wesley are good examples.

As a person begins to develop his true potential, a new group of motivating needs surface—these cluster around *the desire to know and understand*. Some of the characteristics of this stage are increased curiosity and a desire to unify one's collected concepts of religion. These people would no doubt want to think about great questions and examine theories concerning their solution. Many professors in graduate work, both theological and secular, appear to be motivated by the need to know and understand. A minister who preaches to the desire to know and understand can soon frustrate his congregation because most of the congregation will be absorbed with other needs such as security, love, and self-esteem. So the preacher needs to shift his preaching to the needs of his people. Dr. Samuel Young gave good counsel when he said, "I never preach my theories."

Finally, Maslow described the top level of *aesthetic needs*. Such a person has a longing for beauty, order, and harmony. Such a person loves truth simply because it is truth and beauty simply because of the joy of experiencing it, not for what either can do for him. Such individuals would simply want to enjoy God forever, not wanting something from Him.

Bringing People's Needs and the Bible Together

Preaching that is not saturated with biblical authority soon deteriorates into a confused commentary on the morass in which we already find ourselves. The thrill for the pastor who believes in the authority of the Scriptures is the assurance that the Holy Spirit can use his proclaiming of the Word to give pulsating rhythm to the whole symphony of needs his people feel. But how can it happen in the week-by-week pulpit work?

Every sermon has two main purposes. First, the preacher should identify the problem. As an example, the preacher may address himself to one of the basic needs or one of the prevalent stress factors of present life such as divorce. Secondly, a positive biblical solution to the problem must be offered.

Soon after a sermon has started, parishioners should recognize their preacher is tackling a vital life concern. He is handling a question, discussing a problem, speaking of a bewildering experience, or identifying a felt need. When a preacher with moderate skill helps the congregation solve their real problems with the Scriptures, he fulfills the role of biblical preaching.

Today's preacher, believing in the authority of the Scriptures, should start with real need and then throw all the light on the problem he can find in the Scriptures. Nothing he says on any subject, however wise or important, matters much unless it makes vital contact with the daily life situations of the congregation. Such sermons will keep people coming back, and they will grow in the coming too.

That a preacher should know the Bible goes without saying, but he may know it ever so well and yet fail to get it within reaching distance of anybody unless he intimately understands people. His greatest concern must be what is happening inside of them. He must really care. Then the sermon becomes "an engineering operation by which a chasm is spanned so that spiritual goods on one side are actually transported into personal lives upon the other."[8]

Life-situation preaching is not preaching on a subject so much as it is preaching to an object. It presents a real problem which calls for a scriptual solution; and the solution is found, not in the persons involved, but in God. It is preaching that starts where people live. When the first grade class in a Detroit school started studying various types of animals, they did more than look at pictures. They spent a day at the Detroit zoo. The teacher directed the children's learning. Effective life-situation preaching does the same thing; spiritual truth is brought to bear on the concerns actually being experienced. It is all wrapped up in John Dewey's dictum that thinking begins with a felt need. Then the sermon sounds like Archibald MacLeish's descriptive phrase—"the sharp, clear stroke when the axe goes into living wood."

Advantages of Life-Situation Preaching

There are advantages to this type of preaching. For one thing, it sharpens the evangelistic edge. It relies on a sharp, particular persuasion rather than a dulled general appeal. To the great words of evangelism, "Repent and believe," it offers the persuasion to turn from some particular destructive way of thinking or acting. The persuasion is to accept Christ at a localized point of need.

This type of preaching also saves from offering vague generalities and preaching practically the same sermon every Sunday. It speaks to vital issues, helps the pastor stay close to human reality, and offers divine assurance in the midst of felt needs.

131

There are several ways in which the minister may discover needs on which he may preach. Three of the best ways is through calling, counseling, and hospital visitation. These ministries should never be viewed as an appendix to preaching, but rather as a vital preparation for preaching. Of course that which is heard in confidence or that which would bring embarrassment is never shared from the pulpit.

Then, too, an alert pastor will become aware of his people's problems as he carries on conversation with them after services. Here he will seek to recognize the deep needs of persons and not just hear their words which often hide these needs.

Another means of discovering needs is through the application of basic principles of psychology. The pastor may find the theories of Alfred Adler, G. A. Allpart, Erich Fromm, and C. G. Jung helpful.

The only way a pastor can really know how a member of his congregation feels is to become that person insofar as he can do that vicariously. Then by means of consecrated imagination, coupled with biblical understanding and positive application, he begins to see viable solutions to the human dilemma.

Often I make a secret retreat during the week to the silent sanctuary of our church to sit in a pew for a period of quiet meditation. There a deep feeling of appreciation for the worshippers in whose place I sit comes to me. These people will be in church next Sunday and will look to me for something to steady them in faltering moments and to help them develop a sturdy faith that will give worth to their lives.

What a challenge! The sense of great issues must be coupled with an equally vivid understanding of people and their predicaments., and a knowledge of the Scriptures and their application to the bewildering range of human needs, if the preacher's preaching is to be vital and effective. Without this, he will become a pulpit piano tuner, striking only one note instead of playing on the whole gospel keyboard.

To us has been given the high, exacting task of interpreting the Word and applying it to people's lives so the full meaning of life in Christ can be felt and understood. Life-situation preaching starts with life where it is. And by applying the Bible to human needs, the preacher introduces his hearers to what Jesus meant life to be.

● Neil B. Wiseman

9

Lay Partnership in Biblical Preaching

First-century believers are examples of the way biblical preaching can powerfully influence the Church in every generation. The eyewitness testimonies which their preachers gladly shared—"I was there and I know"—added enormous clout to their life-changing preaching. Those new converts were shaped and changed by the proclamation of the truth.

At Nazareth in His hometown synagogue, Jesus preached the prophecies of Isaiah; on an ordinary hillside, more than 5,000 listened intently to Him and forgot their need of food; and in a wide variety of smaller groups, He made truth understandable with a simple parable. Peter's preaching is recorded in several settings; and on one occasion his proclamation was so gripping that his listeners cried, "What must we do?"

134

And Paul planted churches with his gospel preaching which took him on wide travels, even to the university debating society on Mars Hill. So important was preaching to Paul that he wrote, "For since, in the wisdom of God, the world did not know God through wisdom, *it pleased God through the folly of what we preach to save those who believe.* For Jews demand signs and Greeks seek wisdom, but we preach Christ crucified, a stumbling block to Jews and folly to Gentiles, but to those who are called, both Jews and Greeks, Christ the power of God and the wisdom of God" (1 Cor. 1:21–24, RSV, italics added).

Paul, the first-century preacher, continues, "When I came to you, brethren, *I did not come proclaiming to you the testimony of God in lofty words of wisdom.* For I decided to know nothing among you except Jesus Christ and him crucified. And I was with you in weakness and in much fear and trembling; and *my speech and my message was not in plausible words of wisdom,* but in demonstration of the spirit and power, that your faith might not rest in the wisdom of men but in the power of God" (1 Cor. 2:1–5, RSV, italics added).

True, preaching in the first century deeply influenced the Early Church. Preaching was supremely important then both to the preacher and the hearer. But isn't our century and generation different?

Poetic description of our century calls it the best and the worst of times. Scientific discovery, quick global communications, efficient travel, emerging nations, unprecedented prosperity next to poverty, and so much more marks this "roller-coaster" period of both aspiration and broken dreams. These first seven decades of this century have been molded by vast social change, a wide variety of developing understandings about man and his world, broken families, justifiable cynicism of governments and the church. Never has a fresh word from God been more needed.

Twentieth-century preaching has been widely publicized. Unusual communication channels have taken preaching to strange places like the steps of the Washington Monument, the White House, football fields, and over national radio and television. But this new image for preaching has done little to increase the influence of the pulpit. Like Eutychus, the famous sermon snoozer of Paul's time, modern man finds 11:20 until 11:55 a.m. on Sundays a good time for napping, a useful period for planning a new week, or a good time to put his mind in neutral because it is tired from a busy, materialistic week.

Preaching is in trouble. Even her best friends wonder if she is critically ill or perhaps even dead.

Turbulent, trying times could cause such a predicament. But could it be that modern man is no longer interested in preaching? And should he be? Has the television age with its instant message, its professional casting, and its deeply moving emotional impact conditioned people to expect a better show than the average cleric produces Sunday by Sunday? Or have preachers lost their nerve? Is the deathly charge of irrelevance accurate?

A preaching assignment recently took me to Atlanta. Nettie, the black motel maid, was fascinated with my speedy, though inaccurate, typing; and I asked her what she thought about preaching. She thought the problem was that ministers are too well educated to understand the real problems in people's lives. "How could they know what is bothering me?" she asked and then admitted that she had not been to church for months.

And only yesterday I heard a layman who knows the church well say, "The preacher never seems to scratch where I itch."

Last Monday I heard a college junior ask how to get a seminary education without losing close contact with the common folks like those back home. Then, too, a self-made preacher recently made a 100-mile trip to our campus to inquire how to apply the Bible to the everyday needs of his congregation.

Two months ago, the lady greeter where I was to be the guest preacher, told me, "Make it short and sweet." As if a fresh word from God would necessarily be either short or sweet.

But preaching still lives in spite of such a distressing environment. Enter any place of worship on any Sunday and you can probably count on hearing a sermon. But how can we make preaching better? Are there ways to make our preaching more meaningful to the people who come to hear us preach? And can we again interest those who have long ago turned us off or deserted the church?

Our options are (1) to "curse the darkness" and let the church settle down in a swampland of mediocrity; or (2) to upgrade our preaching so as to get the message through to our hearers until lives are transformed and hope is born anew. Clyde E. Fant succinctly states the issue: "We must be committed to the historical word and the contemporary world. Without the word we have no message. Without the world we have no ministry."[1]

1. Dialogical or Cooperative Preaching

The present-day preacher must come to grips with this age. Newsmagazines, novels, newspapers, and the TV documentaries will help; but to really understand these times, the minister must be in meaningful conversation with his people. Deeper than clergy-church member chitchat, he must hear them asking the deepest questions of human existence. He must be aware that serious people

137

of this age are trying to figure out what life is all about. He should know that some sermon listeners do not understand what one of them called "God talk" and another called "religious mumbo jumbo."

Some parishioners think we preachers do not know the real issues. Other people of the pews think we are afraid to tackle hard questions and controversial issues. While still other church attenders think we use heavenly jargon with no earthly sense. Hopefully such suspicions are inaccurate or overstated. But how will our hearers change their minds unless we have serious conversations with them about preaching? And how do they tell us what we need to hear about preaching?

Many recent books on preaching suggest that a partial answer is found in *dialogical preaching*. Perhaps the term *cooperative preaching* is more precise. But dialogical preaching need not go to the extremes of having a parishioner and the preacher in actual conversation during the sermon. To many contemporary worshippers that would be disturbing. How then is dialogical input received by the preacher?

a. The Unfinished or Open-ended Sermon

In the college chapel, I sometimes truthfully testify that I have studied, prayed, and prepared for this sermon. Then I proceed to share my discoveries, but I openly admit that I do not see in the passage all the life ramifications for a college student. For example, I have used as a text the demand of Jesus, "If any man will come after me, let him deny himself, and take up his cross daily, and follow me" (Luke 9:23). After careful exegetical and expository work, I ask, "What does this scripture say to you today?" Then I ask the students to live the passage and to share their insights with me. Each time I try such a method, 10 or more students wait to talk with me, some write notes of commitment, and others come to my office.

Of course, it is somewhat damaging to one's self-image to admit to 800 students that my sermon is unfinished; but really, every sermon is unfinished until it is applied to life by someone. But how exciting it is to actually experience people applying the scripture to life in ways which reach beyond the preacher's understanding of the passage. Then, too, as they share, the preacher gets an inside track on his people's thoughts and experiences—an enriching preparation for future preaching.

b. The Previous Conversation Approach

Good input for preaching comes from discussing a scripture passage with a select group of parishioners before one does the preaching. One pastor frequently meets four to six of his church members for a Tuesday lunch to discuss next Sunday's sermon. If good ideas arise from one mind, think how many more would come from several! For example, he might discuss his plan to preach on the new birth next Sunday. He can ask his luncheon group what the doctrine means to them, when they first heard this doctrine, and when they experienced the forgiveness of God. In such conversations the strengths, weaknesses, errors, and experiences of the parishioners will give valuable direction and enhance both preparation and proclamation. And think of the spiritual camaraderie between pulpit and pew when the preacher begins to preach such a cooperative sermon.

Dow Kirkpatrick is right:

I am a preacher. There have been times when I thought I wanted to break down the walls and enter the layman's world, but I never figured out how. . . . When I listen to other people talk about their worlds, I discover *everyone* lives in an ivory tower of his own

139

kind.... We need, not to escape from our world for some kind of inauthentic entrance into another, but we need each other.[2]

From this concept Kirkpatrick developed a helpful plan. A small group of laymen in a specific vocation were invited to two discussions with the pastor in which the conversation topic revolved around ways the Christian faith could help them in the real issues which faced them in their six-day world. In his church, Kirkpatrick met with physicians, lawyers, businessmen, ministers, scientists, civil servants, and retirees. But the idea could very well be expanded to teen-agers, newly married couples, schoolteachers—the possibilities are exhaustless. Those who have tried such approaches find strong complaints from parishioners who were left out of a discussion group—a kind of negative approval of the technique.

c. The After-Sermon Question Approach

Preaching might be revolutionized by providing the layman a simple opportunity to ask the preacher, "What do you mean?" The possibility of such a question might help all of us who try to preach to be more clear, concise, and concrete. And affording such an opportunity might make our hearers more alert and prompt tough, thoughtful questions. Both ways preaching is improved.

This can be done in an after-service setting. In some churches such a discussion could be held in the sanctuary; but since few people are accustomed to "talk back" to the preacher there, it is probably better to take the discussion to a Sunday school classroom or the fellowship hall. Then no one need feel obligated to remain for pew-to-pulpit dialogue. But the especially alert preacher might want to judge the relevancy of his preaching by how many people stay to talk about it.

One Arkansas congregation uses the Wednesday evening service for pastor and congregation dialogue about the morning sermon from the previous Sunday. Obviously this arrangement would not be used every week; but when it is to be used, the pastor announces his Wednesday plan in the Sunday bulletin, asking the congregation to bring their questions and personal insights. The pastor reports, "If not overdone, it makes for lively discussion and surprising insights by our laymen."

d. The Parishioner Perspective Approach

One of the best-known preachers of this century, Harry Emerson Fosdick, had a useful device that always captured his hearers' attention. About halfway through a sermon, after building an impressive case like the trial lawyer, he would often say, "But some of you have not found this to be true in your life." Then he would preach his main ideas again as if he were sitting in the pew. From the perspective of the parishioner he would anticipate their hard questions and deal with them. That approach, while never in direct public conversation with a church member, keeps the hearer with the preacher all the way. As Thor Hall puts it, it forces the preacher "to involve himself with others in the consideration of the deepest levels of existence and meaning."[3] And that sounds like Donald G. Miller's idea:

> The Incarnation, the Cross, and the Resurrection together are parts of the one grand event before which the whole universe is brought to judgment and offered grace... Through the retelling of the story, the whole event must be "placarded," reenacted before the eyes of each successive generation, until they become living participants in both its judgment and its grace.[4]

A simple beginning for cooperative preaching is for the proclaimer to have an imaginary dialogue in his own mind with his hearers. He might very well ask himself if he had recently suffered bereavement, what he would need to hear from the Word of God. Or if he had had a teen-ager who had experimented with drugs last week, what would he need from the man of God? And if he had cut corners on his tax return, what demanding word would he need to hear preached? Bonhoeffer insisted, "It is characteristic of the preacher that he simultaneously questions and proclaims. He must ask along with the congregation, and form a 'Socratic' community, otherwise he could not give a reply."[5]

e. Home Visitation

Many preachers have nearly quit routine home visitation of their parishioners, and in some places the people have hardly missed the calling cleric. Could it be that preachers have quit and parishioners have hardly missed the calls because so little has happened in previous house-to-house visitations? Modern people are hard to find at home; and when they are home, they are bored by a caller who only dutifully talks of "safe" subjects. After the weather, the growth of the children, the new furniture, and a word or two about family members, the conversation is about over; so we had better pray and, if it seems reasonably appropriate, read some scripture.

But why not use those calls to talk about preaching? The questions might go like this: "What did the sermon say to you?" "Did you receive any helpful new insights into the Scriptures during the sermon Sunday? If so, what?" "What should I consider preaching in the future?" or "What sermon moved you most in all your Christian life?"

After the initial comment, "Pastor, that was the best sermon I have ever heard," the conversation may lag and the silence may be deafening. But when the people are convinced that we really want to hear what preaching is doing in their lives and we want to preach better, they will share their hurts and burdens with us. The results—they will be better sermon hearers and we preachers will preach better because of their insights.

Never satisfied with his understandings of God and man, the preacher must live with the demanding but creative tension of the street and the study. In the study with his Bible, his books, and his quiet time, the preacher must feel the pull of the people out in the real world. And when he is among the people, he feels the drawing power of the study. The effective preacher is a man of both worlds. Abbey is right, "Both the personal care of a concerned pastor and the pulpit guidance of a wise preacher are needed, and in the minister's day-to-day work the two functions support each other."[6]

Preachers for these times must celebrate both the joys of their people and feel deeply with the grief sufferer. These caring preachers live out their sermons with the lonely, the old, the hurting, and also the happy. The credible proclaimer seeks to offer the grace of God for individual sin, to appropriately whisper or thunder the prophetic word in the social arena of human existence, and to significantly identify with both the hilarious and the hurting. Modern man needs such a preacher, and some dialogue between proclaimer and hearer makes these relationships productive.

f. Cooperative Preaching—a Biblical Method

Preaching methods in the New Testament were often

very different from the lecture, monological sermon of to-day. Lloyd M. Perry explains:

> Preaching (in the New Testament) consisted of reading a passage of Scripture followed by clarification or exposition. In the services, any qualified person was permitted to speak, to argue, or to discuss. Jesus preached few sermons patterned after our conventional sermons which are preached today. Of some 125 incidents recorded in the gospels wherein Jesus communicated with people, about 54 percent were initiated by the auditors. His communication was characterized by a conversation with questions and answers, objections, debate, agreement and rejection.[7]

And William Thompson, in his interesting book, *A Listener's Guide to Preaching*, says, "It did not occur to the very first Christians to delegate the responsibility for preaching or officiating in worship exclusively to one of their members. The entire church shared the responsibility."[8]

The whole issue behind dialogical-cooperative preaching is summarized by Clyde Reid as follows:

> One of the great dilemmas in the present pattern of the church life is the sheer volume of information we present to our congregations. Week after week, we load them with additional ideas, concepts, duties, and responsibilities, with no opportunity to talk back, to wrestle with those ideas, to absorb and integrate the content before we dump some more. It is little wonder that the seed lies on the top of the ground and does not put down roots in the lives of the listeners.[9]

He is right! Attempts at cooperative preaching will improve the situation.

2. Worthwhile Preaching

If preaching is dying, or at least seriously ill, it can easily be revived with worthwhile preaching. The verdict of my friend and former professor, John Killinger, is correct: "People are not tired of preaching but of non-preaching, of badly garbled, irrelevant drivel that has in so many places passed for preaching because there was no real preaching to measure it against."[10] To waste one's preaching time is to stand judged by God. And every arid, barren, lifeless sermon is a disgrace to the preacher and an embarrassment to the listener. Preaching must be worthy of a hearing.

To make preaching worthwhile, it must be understood; an awareness of the communication process is needed. Like falling rain, new books on the process and art of communication are being produced. Lycurgus M. Starkey, Jr., says, "Television and stereo are the confirmation class par excellence for our adolescents in their rite of passage to moral maturity."[11] Given the modern environment which fairly crackles with interesting communication, plus the limitations of time and space imposed by the short sermon and the modern pulpit, the twentieth-century preacher must work doubly hard at sharpening his communication skills.

New materials for improved communication are readily available. But improvement requires constant study of the developing data. Modern communication research must be interpreted so preachers can fully understand both the possibilities of improved communication and the vast liabilities of faulty communication. Thor Hall says:

> The study of communications media belongs inextricably within the ecology of homiletics, and the

new frontiers of knowledge and thought that appear in this area are of as much significance for those who seek to understand the nature and practice of preaching as for those engaged in teaching, acting, broadcasting, performing, or entertaining.[12]

Elton Trueblood concisely states the issue: "Though the time when it was easy to assemble a crowd is over, at least for the immediate present, it is still true that people will gather where they have reason to believe that something will be said, with clarity and conviction, about life's most important issues."[13]

3. Applied Preaching

Teachers of preaching push their students to deal with exegesis, exposition, and application. And frequently the student fails to see these three parts of preaching as a necessity for effective, long-range pulpit work. Recently students have seemed to be helped by putting these three parts into time sequences. (1) The *exegesis* becomes the *then* of the biblical record, and the questions are: Why was this written? What does it really say? Whom did the writer address? What did he mean? (2) The *exposition* has to do with the *always*. It seeks to find the universal truth of a given passage of scripture. Here the question, simply stated, is: What does the passage say to everyone, everywhere, in every generation? (3) The third time dimension—*now*—deals with the *application* of a passage to people of this present generation.

Application is the preacher's work of making God's truth understood, relevant, and meaningful to contemporary man; it is never finished until the listener knows what he can do about the proclaimed truth. Spurgeon said the sermon really begins when application begins.

Perhaps the most devastating comment ever made on

a preacher's sermon is "So what?" But the question is right and it should push and pull at every sermon. J. W. Etter said that preaching without application is like the physician giving the sick man a lecture on health without writing a prescription.[14]

Modern, well-dressed, informed, apparently sophisticated people are frequently spiritually illiterate. Thus their preacher cannot allow himself the luxury of assuming that his hearers know how to apply truth. The modern person is usually well educated, but his knowledge is fragmented, dissociated, competing, and in narrowly specialized fields. Thus contemporary man is often a long way from adequately understanding the faith. Fred B. Craddock explains our dilemma:

> The plain fact of the matter is that we are seeking to communicate with people whose experiences are concrete.... No farmer deals with the problem of calfhood, only with the calf. The woman in the kitchen is not occupied with the culinary arts in general but with a particular roast or cake. The wood craftsman is hardly able to discuss intelligently the topic of "chairness," but he is a master with a chair.... The minister says "all men are mortal" and meets drowsy agreement; he announces that "Mr. Brown's son is dying" and the church becomes the church.[15]

Laity need and respond to biblical truth spoken in plain speech with love. Windy cliches, big words, and foggy sentence constructions will probably be tolerated by our long suffering hearers, but profound truth spoken simply and applied to life will lead them to saving faith and/or challenge them to total commitment.

4. Candor in Preaching

Sound biblical preaching is constructed on two basic New Testament confessions. Simon's clear affirmation,

147

"Thou art the Christ, the Son of the living God" (Matt. 16:16), is the foundation premise of all Christian preaching. But a life motto from all preachers comes from Paul's announcement at Lystra, *"We are only human beings, no less mortal than you.* The good news we bring tells you to turn from your follies to the living God, who made heaven and earth and sea and everything in them" (Acts 14:16, NEB, italics added). In the high moments, the low moments, and all the in-between moments, the preacher must build his ministry on those two confessions—"Thou art the Christ" and "We are human beings."

Elsewhere in this book, there is a correct and needed emphasis on the first confession. But a word about the second confession is needed too. The preacher is a human being forgiven by the grace of God and called to preach; he is no miniature god or super-saint. Preachers who pretend to be supermen or extraordinary Christians live a miserable existence. And playacting, masquerading, pretense, and image building are a senseless waste of energy—the stuff out of which boredom, frustration, and despair are made.

Preachers, being mortal, are not divine. And this humanity needs to be admitted freely to contemporary congregations. It is self-destructive to create an image of being a wizard when one is only a 90-day statistical wonder. It is phony to pose as a charter member of the eternal happiness club—the cult with the big, empty smile—when hurt and loneliness gnaw at one's heart. It is playacting to toot one's integrity while manipulating church members for one's own interest. Pretense hurts preaching—it always has and it always will.

Because of his humanness, the preacher is able to identify significantly with individuals in his congregation. Thus the only appropriate stance for the Christian preacher is to join D. T. Niles when he said, "I am a sinner for whom Christ died. I am just one of those who has been loved by God in Jesus at the cross. That is the central truth about me. All the rest is peripheral."[16]

But curiously enough, when a preacher admits his own humanness, his congregation often finds new credibility in his preaching; he is more believable. Then they identify with the preacher with their simple "me too" as an honest response to his message. Such openness and honesty on the preacher's part may provoke a display of hostility and alienation from sick souls and neurotic personalities. But the great host of sermon listeners will view such an admission of common ground as a valuable opportunity for them to really see God at work in a live, honest human being—their preacher. The superman idea is unmasked for the horrible falsehood that it is, and the grace of God is exalted for what it is.

But how? It can be accomplished in many ways. Once it happened in my classroom on the college campus. In our family a close relative lay dying with terminal cancer. In seeking to apply the grace of God to the first death in our family, I found myself asking some eternal questions. To that class of ministerial students I admitted, "I hurt and I have deep questions. Someone else will have to pray today." Spontaneously one of the class members began to pray for me and my family. Following the prayer another student testified that he had been praying for me daily. Both the prayer and the testimony became means of grace to me. But beyond that was the authentic, common ground for teaching and preaching that was established between them and me.

It is not the lengthy recitation of past, forgiven sins that makes a congregation believe we are human. It most often shows itself in such self-revealing statements as "I

149

need prayers"; "Sometimes it is hard to be a good parent"; "Having family devotions is difficult at our house"; or "Adversity is sometimes hard for me to understand."

Conversely, nonhuman and unrealistic statements sound like this: "My wife and I have never had a disagreement"; "I have never felt any hostility or anger since being saved"; "A sanctified Christian has no feelings"; or "Suffering and death are not a problem to the real Christian."

Authentic Bible preaching is done by the preacher who stations himself midpoint between the biblical record and contemporary man. Such a preacher is in phase with life as it is. And in his own humanness he shows himself as being in touch with reality. With candor and honesty he allows his people to see into his soul, to see his humanness, and to see that he is on a lifelong spiritual journey. To the present moment that adventuresome pilgrimage has taken him through valleys, to mountain peaks, across arid plains, and through fruitful orchards.

Since he is on a journey, he is able to report some progress and to frankly admit with the popular poster, "Be patient with me. God ain't through with me yet." With such a stance the preacher can transform tragedies into teachers and thorns into testimonies to the grace of God. Then his preaching which is lived out in daily existence in his parish will be a redemptive example of Karl Barth's idea that "we are worthy of being believed only as we are aware of our unworthiness."[17]

People in the pews always have a kind of spiritual restlessness when preaching is in the conceptual, theoretical, abstract realms of the far away and long ago. But the candor of self-revelation makes preaching come alive, like Kierkegaard's idea of going to see a religious drama with every intention of being a spectator. Then the chief actor, who represents God, steps to the front of the stage, points his finger, and says, "I want you to take the leading part in this play." That is what our listeners need to sense in our preaching. They need to know that God is calling them to play a leading part in His redemptive plan. There needs to be a personalizing of the message so the obvious conclusion is "God meant that for me!" It is easier for the parishioner to put himself in that position when he has seen the grace of God at work in his preacher.

5. Why Involve Laymen in Preaching?

God's purpose for preaching is to make His message understandable to man. The Bible provides the message. The preacher is the vehicle through which the message travels. But there is no preaching until the message is grasped by the individual. Even the preacher's most profound ideas are worthless until they have practical significance for people. So the whole purpose of lay partnership in preaching is never to take an opinion poll to determine what they want to hear preached. It is rather to involve them significantly in preaching so they will know your preaching is true to the Bible and true to life.

This partnership between listener and preacher makes it possible for both of them to conclude with Wingren, "When the Bible lies open on the preacher's desk and the preparation of the sermon is about to begin, the worshipers have already come in; the passage contains these people since it is God's word to His people."[18] And one might add, the people—our target for preaching—are already there in the mind of the preacher because he has been in meaningful dialogue with them, and his questions concerning the biblical passage are their questions too.

This common ground between preacher and parishioner is explained by Clyde E. Fant: "Preaching is

151

not telling someone what to do; *it is a mutual hearing of the word of God*, as both speaker and listener stand beneath its truth."[19] Such interaction of preacher and laity around the Bible will make preaching as powerful in this century as it was in the Early Church.

About the Authors

RANDAL E. DENNY is pastor of the historic Los Angeles First Church of the Nazarene, which was founded by Phineas F. Bresee. Two books of his sermons have been published: *Tables of Stone for Modern Living*, an exposition of the Ten Commandments; and *The Habit of Happiness*, a study of the Beatitudes. He has for many years disciplined his sermon preparation by developing full manuscript for his Sunday morning sermons.

LESLIE EVANS is pastor of the First Church of the Nazarene, Sheffield, Yorkshire, England. He has served local congregations in the British Isles for 20 years. One who knows both preaching and Evans, said of him, "He is a preacher of great ability and penetration."

ROSS W. HAYSLIP is pastor of the Tucson, Ariz., First Church of the Nazarene, a congregation which he has served for 11 years. He is a lifelong churchman, having served various churches as pastor and on a variety of district committees and college boards. He presently serves the denomination as a member of the General Board, representing the Southwestern Zone. He has written widely for Nazarene and other evangelical publications.

DARRELL E. LUTHER is pastor of Detroit First Church of the Nazarene. He has served various congregations as pastor for 20 years. His graduate work in counseling and family ecology shows through in his preaching and in his writings about preaching. He has written a series of articles on interpersonal relationships for the *Herald of Holiness* titled "Dimension-Adventures in Self-discovery."

WILLIAM E. McCUMBER is college pastor and chairman of the Department of Religion at Eastern Nazarene College. He has authored five books and has served several local churches as pastor for 26 years. Before going to Eastern Nazarene College, he taught at Pasadena College for five years. He has preached across the denomination in revivals, camp meetings, preachers meetings, and holiness conventions.

W. T. PURKISER serves as professor of biblical theology at Point Loma College, San Diego, Calif. He is former editor of the *Herald of Holiness*. Throughout his prolific ministry as writer, editor, teacher, pastor, and administrator, he has always been a gifted preacher of the Word in Bible conferences, camp meetings, servicemen's retreats, local church revivals, and in the chapel services of the educational institutions of the church. His writings include *The Gifts of the Spirit, The New Testament Image of the Ministry, Adventures in Truth, Beliefs That Matter Most, Know Your Old Testament, Security: the False and the True*, and *Conflicting Concepts of Holiness*.

MILLARD REED is senior pastor of Nashville First Church of the Nazarene, the mother church of the denomination in the Southeast. He presently serves the denomination as a member of the board of trustees of Nazarene Theological Seminary. His writings have appeared in church periodicals, and he has authored two books. He is well loved by his congregation for his effective pulpit ministry.

NEIL B. WISEMAN is college chaplain and chairman of the Department of Religion at Trevecca Nazarene College. He has served local churches for 15 years. Although he is deeply interested in Christian education, pastoral training, and urban ministries, preaching is his first love. He is founding director of PALCON, a series of pastoral development conferences for all Nazarene pastors.

MILDRED BANGS WYNKOOP is theologian in residence at Nazarene Theological Seminary in Kansas City. Her writings include *John Wesley, Christian Revolutionary*; *Foundations of Wesleyan-Arminian Theology*; *A Theology of Love*; *The Occult and the Supernatural*; and *The Trevecca Story*. Her ministerial achievements include past president of the Wesleyan Theological Society, distinguished college professor, president of Japan Theological Seminary, and founder of the missions department at Trevecca Nazarene College. But in all her service to the church, she has always been a preacher of the Bible and to the present is one of the most popular chapel preachers on Nazarene college campuses.

Reference Notes

1. WHAT IS BIBLICAL PREACHING? (*W. T. Purkiser*)

1. Peter T. Forsyth, *Positive Preaching and the Modern Mind* (New York: George H. Doran Co., 1907); Herbert H. Farmer, *The Servant of the Word* (New York: Charles Scribner's Sons, 1942); James S. Stewart, *Heralds of God* (New York: Charles Scribner's Sons, 1946) and *A Faith to Proclaim* (New York: Charles Scribner's Sons, 1953); Donald G. Miller, *Fire in Thy Mouth* (New York: Abingdon Press, 1954) and *The Way to Biblical Preaching* (New York: Abingdon Press, 1957); John Knox, *The Integrity of Preaching* (New York: Abingdon Press, 1957).

2. R. E. O. White, *A Guide to Preaching* (Grand Rapids, Mich.: William B. Eerdmans Publishing Co., 1973), p. 32.

3. Georgia Harkness in James Dalton Morrison, ed., *Masterpieces of Religious Verse* (New York: Harper and Brothers Publishers, 1948), No. 1489.

2. RESPONSIBLE BIBLICAL INTERPRETATION (*Mildred Bangs Wynkoop*)

1. Morton Enslin, "Religion Without Theology," *Religion in Life*, spring, 1976, p. 69.

2. James Earl Massey, *The Responsible Pulpit* (Anderson, Ind.: Warner Press, 1974), pp. 53–54.

3. Jay Williams, "Exegesis/Eisegesis: Is There a Difference?" *Theology Today*, October, 1973.

4. W. E. Sangster, *Why Jesus Never Wrote a Book* (London: Epworth Press, 1952).

5. Leander Keck, "Listening To and Listening For," *Interpretation* magazine, April, 1973.

6. Walter Wink, "How I Have Been Snagged by the Seat of My Pants While Reading the Bible," *Christian Century*, Sept. 24, 1975.

7. John Wesley, "Address to the Clergy," February, 1756.

8. C. Peter Wagner, "Bibliolatry," *Eternity* magazine, November, 1958, p. 16.

9. Enslin, *Religion in Life*, p. 70.

10. Henry H. Mitchell, *Black Preaching* (New York: Lippincott Press, 1970), p. 35.

11. James Smart, *The Strange Silence of the Bible in the Church* (Philadelphia: Westminster Press, 1970), p. 163.

12. Mitchell, *Black Preaching*, p. 30.

3. PREACHING GREAT PARAGRAPHS (*W. E. McCumber*)
   No reference notes

4. PREACHING GREAT BIBLE BOOKS (*Randal E. Denny*)

1. Alan M. Stibbs, *Expounding God's Word* (Grand Rapids, Mich.: Wm. B. Eerdmans Publishing Co., 1961), p. 18.

2. James S. Stewart, *Heralds of God* (New York: Charles Scribner's Sons, 1956), p. 166.

3. Andrew Blackwood, *The Preparation of Sermons* (New York: Abingdon Press, 1958), p. 71.

4. William Barclay, *Communicating the Gospel* (Nashville: The Upper Room, 1971), pp. 34–35.

5. Dwight E. Stevenson, *Preaching on the Books of the Old Testament* (New York: Harper and Brothers, Publishers, 1956), p. 11.

6. *Ibid.*, p. 259.

7. Donald G. Miller, *The Way to Biblical Preaching* (New York: Abingdon Press, 1957), p.40.

8. Stevenson, *Preaching on the Books of the OT*, p. 14.

9. Andrew W. Blackwood, *Preaching from the Bible* (New York: Abingdon-Cokesbury Press, 1941), p. 170.

10. Harold Elkin Knott, *How to Prepare an Expository Sermon* (Cincinnati: Standard Publishing Co., 1930), p. 32.

11. Stevenson, *Preaching on the Books of the OT*, p. 13.

12. *Ibid.*

13. Miller, *Biblical Preaching*, p. 96.

14. Henry Clayton Mark, *Patterns for Preaching: The Art of Sermon Making* (Grand Rapids, Mich.: Zondervan Publishing House, 1959), p. 153.

15. *Ibid.*, p. 155.

16. *Ibid.*, p. 156.

17. *Ibid.*, p. 158.

18. J. Glenn Gould, *Healing the Hurt of Man* (Kansas City: Beacon Hill Press of Kansas City, 1971), p. 60.

19. Stibbs, *Expounding God's Word*, pp. 36–37.

20. Andrew W. Blackwood, *Preaching from Prophetic Books* (New York: Abingdon-Cokesbury Press, 1951), p. 194.

21. W. A. Criswell, "Preaching Through The Bible," *Christianity Today* (Dec. 9, 1966), p. 19.

22. Miller, *Biblical Preaching*, p. 42.

23. Knott, *How to Prepare*, pp. 36–37.

24. Blackwood, *Preaching from Prophetic Books*, p. 200.

25. Miller, *Biblical Preaching*, p. 53.

5. PEACHING GREAT BIBLE CHARACTERS (*Ross W. Hayslip*)

1. Frank H. Caldwell, *Preaching Angles* (Nashville: Abingdon Press, 1954), pp. 54–55.

2. Andrew W. Blackwood, *Preaching from the Bible* (Nashville: Abingdon Press, 1941), p. 63.

3. Baumann, *Introduction to Contemporary Preaching* (Grand Rapids, Mich.: Baker Book House, 1972), p. 251.

4. Paul S. Rees, *Men of Action in Acts* (Westwood, N.J.: Fleming H. Revell Co., 1966), p. vii.

5. J. Sidlow Baxter, *Mark These Men* (Grand Rapids, Mich.: Zondervan Publishing House, 1960), p. 5.

6. PREACHING GREAT BIBLICAL EVENTS (*Millard Reed*)

1. George E. Sweazey, *Preaching the Good News* (Englewood Cliffs, N.J.: Prentice-Hall, Inc., 1976), p. 59.

2. *Ibid.*

3. Karl Barth, *The Preaching of the Gospel* (Philadelphia: Westminster Press, 1963), p. 17.

4. *Ibid.*, p. 9.

5. James S. Stewart, *A Faith to Proclaim* (New York: Charles Scribner's Sons, 1953), pp. 11–47.

6. Jurgen Moltmann, *The Crucified God* (New York: Harper and Row, 1973), p. 1.

7. Stewart, *Faith to Proclaim*, p. 95.

8. *Ibid.*

9. Emil Brunner, *The Christian Doctrine of Creation and Redemption* (Philadelphia: Westminster Press, 1952), p. 9.

10. Langdon Gilkey, *Maker of Heaven and Earth* (Garden City, N.Y.: Doubleday and Co., Inc., 1959), pp. 13 ff.

7. PREACHING GREAT BIBLICAL DOCTRINES (*Leslie Evans*)

1. John A. Broadus, *Preparation and Delivery of Sermons* (London: Hodder and Stoughton, 1905), p. 76.

2. Lloyd M. Perry, *Biblical Preaching for Today's World* (Chicago: Moody Press, 1973), p. 127.

3. J. W. Alexander, *Thoughts on Preaching* (Edinburgh: The Banner of Truth Trust, 1975), p. 214.

4. William Barclay, *The Epistles to Timothy and Titus* (Edinburgh: The Church of Scotland, 1956), p. 77.

5. David Sheppard, *Parson's Pitch* (London: Hodder and Stoughton, 1964), p. 48.

6. James S. Stewart, *A Faith to Proclaim* (London: Hodder and Stoughton, 1953), p. 31.

7. W. E. Sangster, *The Craft of the Sermon* (London: The Epworth Press, 1954), p. 34.

8. Henry Sloan Coffin, *What to Preach* (New York: Harper and Brothers, 1926), p. 48.

9. *Doctrinal Preaching* (London: The Methodist Local Preachers Department, 1951), p. 9.

10. Norman G. Dunning, *Samuel Chadwick* (London: Hodder and Stoughton, 1933), p. 82.

11. Sangster, *Craft of the Sermon*, p. 34.

12. Ilion T. Jones, *Principles and Practice of Preaching* (London: Independent Press, Ltd., 1958), p. 37.

13. Cleverley Ford, *A Theological Preacher's Notebook* (London: Hodder and Stoughton, 1963), pp. 18–19.

14. A. W. Tozer, *Of God and Men* (Harrisburg, Pa.: Christian Publications, Inc., 1960), pp. 26–27.

15. James Stalker, *The Preacher and His Models* (London: Hodder and Stoughton, 1892), p. 256.

16. James S. Stewart, *The Strong Name* (Edinburgh: T. and T. Clark, 1940), pp. 46–57.

17. Ian Macpherson, *None Other Name* (London: The Epworth Press, 1946), pp. 77–84.

18. W. E. Sangster, *Power in Preaching* (London: The Epworth Press, 1958), pp. 41–43.

8. MAKING LIFE-SITUATION PREACHING BIBLICAL (*Darrell E. Luther*)

1. Faris Whitesell, *Power in Expository Preaching* (Westwood, N.J.: Fleming H. Revell Co., 1963).

2. Paul Schere, *The Word God Sent* (New York: Harper and Row, 1965).

3. Karl Barth, *The Word of God and the Word of Man* (Boston: The Pilgrim Press, 1928).

4. J. B. Phillips, *The Ring of Truth* (New York: The Macmillan Co., 1967).

5. J. L. Tizard, *Preaching: the Art of Communication* (London: Oxford University Press, 1958).

6. *Time* magazine (March 1, 1971).

7. Abraham Maslow, *Motivation and Human Behavior*, rev. ed. (New York: Harper and Row, 1970).

8. Harry Emerson Fosdick, *The Art of Preaching*.

9. LAY PARTNERSHIP IN BIBLICAL PREACHING (*Neil B. Wiseman*)

1. Clyde E. Fant, *Preaching for Today* (New York: Harper and Row, 1975), p. 55.

2. Dow Kirkpatrick, *Six Days–and Sunday* (Nashville: Abingdon Press, 1968), p. 5.

3. Thor Hall, *The Future Shape of Preaching* (Philadelphia: Fortress Press, 1971), p. 127.

4. Donald G. Miller, *The Way to Biblical Preaching* (New York: Abingdon Press, 1957), p. 15.

5. Fant, *Preaching for Today*, p. 176.

6. Merrill R. Abbey, *Communication in Pulpit and Parish* (Philadelphia: Westminster Press, 1973), p. 129.

7. Lloyd M. Perry, *Biblical Preaching for Today's World* (Chicago: Moody Press, 1973), p. 96.

8. William Thompson, *A Listener's Guide to Preaching* (New York: Abingdon Press, 1966), p. 32.

9. Clyde Reid, *The Empty Pulpit* (New York: Harper and Row, 1967), p. 90.

10. John Killinger, *The Centrality of Preaching in the Total Task of the Ministry* (Waco, Tex.: Word Books, 1969), p. 21.

11. Abbey, *Communication*, p. 36.

12. Hall, *Future Shape of Preaching*, p. 4.

13. Elton Trueblood, *The Incendiary Fellowship* (New York: Harper and Row, 1967), p. 48.

14. J. W. Etter, *The Preacher and His Sermon* (Dayton, Ohio: United Brethren, 1883), p. 372.

15. Fred B. Craddock, *As One Without Authority* (Enid, Okla.: Phillips University Press, 1974), p. 60.

16. D. T. Niles, *Preaching the Gospel of the Resurrection* (Philadelphia: Westminster Press, 1953), p. 45.

17. Karl Barth, *The Word of God and the Word of Man* (New York: Harper and Brothers, 1957), p. 129.

18. Gustaf Wingren, *The Living Word* (Philadelphia: Fortress Press, 1960), p. 26.

19. Fant, *Preaching for Today*, p. 174.